Nathaniel Dimock

Testimonies of English Divines

Nathaniel Dimock

Testimonies of English Divines

ISBN/EAN: 9783744755047

Printed in Europe, USA, Canada, Australia, Japan

Cover: Foto ©Lupo / pixelio.de

More available books at **www.hansebooks.com**

TESTIMONIES

OF

ENGLISH DIVINES

IN RESPECT OF THE CLAIM OF THE

'MASSING-PRIESTS'

TO OFFER CHRIST FOR THE QUICK AND THE DEAD
TO HAVE REMISSION OF PAIN OR GUILT;

WITH AN INTRODUCTION
BY THE
REV. N. DIMOCK, A.M.

LONDON:
ELLIOT STOCK, 62, PATERNOSTER ROW, E.C.
1896.

CONTENTS.

	PAGE
INTRODUCTION	1
SUPPLEMENTAL POSTSCRIPT	43
TESTIMONIES OF ENGLISH DIVINES	73
APPENDIX	225
NOTE A. — ON THE PUBLICATION OF ÆLFRIC'S HOMILY BY ARCHBISHOP PARKER	225
NOTE B.—ON THE TWO DISTINCT SENSES OF THE VERB 'TO OFFER'	228
NOTE C.—ON THE MASS-DOCTRINE OF SALMERON	236
INDEX	243

TESTIMONIES OF ENGLISH DIVINES
Concerning the Mass-Sacrifice.

INTRODUCTION.

The purpose of the following compilation is to show the contrast between the tradition of the English Reformed Church and the doctrine which is unhappily being loudly proclaimed by some in her name.

There are those among us who are learning to think and to say, 'There has always in the Church of England been a party opposed to Puritanism. Why should we not be willing to welcome such a party now? We cannot make nice distinctions.'

But it is confidently believed that this publication will suffice to show that it needs no eye for nice distinctions to see a chasm deep and broad separating between the doctrines taught by esteemed divines of all sections in the English Church aforetime, and the views propounded by some modern innovators who would willingly seek shelter for themselves under their great names.

Some little pains has been taken to give prominence to writers of the Laudian and non-juring schools of thought. And some divines have been quoted for whose opinions the compiler would not desire to hold a brief.

But we have here nothing to do with questions (however important) at issue between differing schools within the comprehension of the Church of England.

We are looking at a doctrine of the Eucharistic sacrifice, which (as I believe has been shown in 'Dangerous Deceits') seems far outside the boundaries of that comprehension, as defined by our Articles in their fair and obvious and only natural interpretation. And my desire has been to give evidence tending to demonstrate that no school of English divines ever took their stand on the Romish side of the chasm which, since the Reformation, has separated us from the doctrine of the Romish Mass.

It would of course be impossible, without a perfectly exhaustive list (which this does not pretend to be), to prove a 'quod semper, quod ubique, quod ab omnibus,' as applied to the theology of the English Church. But it is believed that no name of any weight and eminence can be produced which can fairly be regarded as an exception to what is here shown to be the rule among our English divines.

In No. 81 of 'Tracts for the Times,' there was given a catena of writers who were cited in support of a new doctrine of the Eucharistic Sacrifice. But not one of these, I believe, will be found to stand on the side of our new teachers.

In saying this, I take no account of the passages quoted as from Bishop Overall, because they are certainly none of his.*

---

* See 'Eucharistic Presence,' pp. 296-298. And it is not easy to believe that they are Cosin's (*ibid.*, p. 297). It must be admitted, I think, even by those who are not fully convinced, that the evidence adduced by Canon Meyrick goes a good way towards proving that they are rather to be attributed to Overall's nephew, J. Hayward. See *Foreign Church Chronicle*, September, 1886, p. 160. See also Mr. Kennion's letter in *Guardian* of October 23, 1889, and especially Canon Meyrick's cogent letters in *Guardian* of October 23, and November 20, 1889, to which may be added his letter in *Guardian* of December 4, 1889.

In years that are past, English Churchmen and representative High Churchmen have not hesitated to denounce the corruptions of Rome, have given assurances for the Protestantism of England's Church, and pledged themselves as supporters of England's Reformation. What would these men say of the doctrines of some who sometimes now make use of their names?

What would the judicious Hooker say, who testified, 'That which they call schism, we know to be our reasonable service unto God and obedience to His voice, which crieth shrill in our ears, "Go out of Babylon, My people, that ye be not partakers of her sins, and that ye receive not of her plagues"'? (Sermon on Jude, Works, vol. iii., p. 675. Edit. Keble.)

What would be said by the bishops and clergy in the time of King James I.?

Perhaps some may be startled at seeing what they did say in the Convocation of 1606. 'If any man shall affirm, under colour of anything that is in the Scriptures, or that can be truly grounded upon natural reason or philosophy, that our Saviour Christ should have showed Himself to have had no discretion, except He had left one chief bishop to have governed all the Churches in the world . . . . or that the intolerable pride of the Bishop of Rome, for the time still being, through the advancement of himself, by many sleights, stratagems, and false miracles, over the Catholic Church (the temple of God), as if he were God Himself, doth not argue him plainly to be the *man of sin* mentioned by the Apostle ; or that every national Church, planted according to the Apostles' platform, may not, by the means which Christ hath ordained, as well subsist of itself, without one universal bishop, as every kingdom may do under the government of their several kings, without one general monarch ; he doth greatly err '* (Cardwell's ' Synodalia,' pp. 377, 379).

What would Bishop Overall say, who has too

---

* Compare the words of Archbishop Parker : ' It is the pride, covetousness, and usurpation of the Bishop of Rome, and of his predecessors, which hath made the princes of the earth to defend their territories and their privileges from that wicked Babylon and her bishop. . . . Thus doth our Reformation detest your Romish errors and heinous presumption. . . . Because ye be so earnest with us of the Reformed Church of these her Majesty's dominions, for often been appealed to, by a strange misapprehension, in support of quasi-Romish error, but who wrote 'Mahomedam sive Turcam, et Papam Romanum simul constituere Anti-Christum est verisimile'? (See 'Eucharistic Presence,' p. 298.)*

What would have been thought by the very learned Joseph Mede, of whom it was said by John Johnson that he 'was not more remark-

---

subjection to foreign tribunals, to confute you and your errors, pray behold and see how we of the Church of England, reformed by our late King Edward and his clergy, and now by her Majesty and hers reviving the same, have but imitated and followed the examples of the ancient and worthy fathers' ('Correspondence,' P.S. edit., pp. 109-111). Similar language concerning the Church of Rome was used by Archbishop Whitgift. See his Works, vol. ii., p. 182, P.S. edit.

On the Canons of 1606 (Overall's 'Convocation Book'), see Cardwell's 'Synodalia,' pp. 330-332. They never had the Royal Assent, the King not liking 'a Convocation entering into such a theory of politics.' But they were passed by both Houses of Convocation.

* See also his words as quoted in p. 302: 'Touching many of which superstitious errors, even the chiefest of them (the same being controverted betwixt us and the Church of Rome), they are discussed in the books ensuing [*i.e.*, the works of Jewel]: and our doctrine is therein justified against the Papists by the certain testimonies of the fathers and constant judgment of antiquity' (in Jewel's Works, P.S. edit., iv., p. 1309).

able for his industry in asserting the Christian sacrifice, than in his laborious proofs that the Church of Rome is the Anti-Christian Church'? (See Tract No. 81, p. 310.)

What would good Bishop Bedell have said? He was a man of most irenical tendencies (see Carr's 'Life of Ussher, p. 227), yet this was his exhortation: 'Intreat them to beware lest they make themselves extremely culpable, not only of partaking with the former *idolatries* . . . but the new detestable doctrines, *Derogatory to the Blood of Christ*, which moderate men even of her own subjects detest: but which she [the Roman Babylon], for fear it should discontent her own creatures and devoted darlings, will not disavow. O if they would fear the plagues of Babylon, and that of all others the fearfulest, *Blindness of mind*, and *strong delusions to believe lies*' (Burnet's 'Life of Bedell,' pp. 167, 168. London, 1685).

What would Bishop Andrewes say? Hear what he did say: 'Vere autem a Torto dicitur, *Romam Christianam* perditam non iri. Non certe, sed *illam quæ inebriata est Sanctorum sanguine, et Martyrum Jesu Christi, Antichristianam* scilicet. Ea enim perdenda est, *cujus in fronte scriptum nomen blasphemiæ* . . . Christi *nomen* deleri oportuit prius, et deletum est, quam *blasphemia*, ibi scriberetur. Postquam autem ibi scripta *blasphemia*, tum demum vere *Babylon* fuit, vere est' ('Tortura Torti,' pp. 220-222, A.C.L.).

What would Bishop Sanderson say, who, speaking of 'the doctrinal errors of the Church of Rome,' says, 'the imposing of these errors upon the consciences of men, to be believed as of necessity, is damnable, and doth not only justify a separation already made, but also bindeth *sub mortali* all true Christians to such a separation' (Works, vol. v., pp. 246, 247. Oxford, 1854); and again, 'Corollaria nonnulla inferam, sed pauca et paucis, merito exosam esse debere cuilibet Christiano Romani Pontificis conjunctam cum summo fastu non ferendam tyrannidem*. . . . Et proinde agnoscendam esse cum omni grati animi significatione summam et singularem Dei Optimi Maximi in nos bonitatem et misericordiam, qui nos patresque nostros et

---

* Compare Sanderson's letter in D'Oyly's 'Life of Sancroft,' vol. i., p. 442.

Ecclesiam Anglicanam tam iniquâ tyrannide dudum exemerit, et justæ libertati quasi postliminio restituerit'? (Vol. iv., pp. 62, 63.)

What would Dr. Hammond say? He wrote, 'I should think all men that have covenanted to reform according to the example of the best reformed Churches, indispensably obliged to conform to the King Edward or Queen Elizabeth English Reformation, the most perfect regular pattern that Europe yieldeth' (Works, vol. i., p. 360. Edit. 1684).*

What would Bishop Jeremy Taylor say? He declared, 'If we will not call them [our Reformers] martyrs, it is clear we have changed our religion since then; and then it should be considered whither we are fallen.' And he adds (in view of Puritan excesses), 'It will be sad to live in an age that should disavow King Edward's and Queen Elizabeth's religion and manner of worshipping God, and in an age that shall do as did Queen Mary's bishops, reject and condemn

---

* It hardly needs to be said that this was written against the purposes of those who desired that the Church of England might be reformed after the model of what they regarded as the 'best reformed' Churches on the Continent.

the Book of Common Prayer, and the religion contained in it' (Works, vol. v., p. 249. Edit. Eden. See 'Papers on Eucharistic Presence,' p. 512).

What would Bishop Bull say, who assures us 'Popery was born and bred in ignorant and unlearned ages; and as soon as learning revived, popery began to decline, till at last the happy Reformation ensued, which we now enjoy' (Works, vol. i., p. 257. Oxford, 1846); and again declares, 'These excellent men, our first reformers, took care to retain and preserve what was primitive and good in the liturgies of other churches, and to pare off all excrescences and adventitious corruptions of after times. . . . We have an entire sacrament, the cup of blessing in the holy Eucharist, which was sacrilegiously taken from us by the Church of Rome, being happily restored to us. The ridiculous pageantry and fopperies of that Church are laid aside, and we have the Holy Sacrament purely, reverently, and decently administered. Let us bless and praise God for these His great mercies, and make a good use of them'? (*Ibid.*, p. 344.)

What would Archbishop Sancroft say? He

desired that the clergy 'take all opportunities of assuring and convincing them [the Protestant Dissenters] that the bishops of this Church are really and sincerely irreconcilable enemies to the errors, superstitions, idolatries, and tyrannies of the Church of Rome, and that the very unkind jealousies which some have had of us to the contrary were altogether groundless. And in the last place, that they warmly and most affectionately exhort them to join with us in daily fervent prayer to the God of Peace for a universal blessed union of all reformed Churches, both at home* and abroad, against our common enemies, and that all they who do confess the Holy Name of our dear Lord, and do agree in the truth of His Holy Word, may also meet in one Holy Communion and live in perfect unity

---

* On Sancroft's 'Scheme of Comprehension,' see D'Oyly's 'Life of Sancroft,' vol. i., pp. 325-330. London: 1821.

In 1678 Sancroft, in conjunction with Bishop Morley, of Winchester, delivered an address to the Duke of York (the design having originated with the bishops) which concluded with these words: 'That Church which teacheth and practiseth the doctrines destructive of salvation is to be relinquished. But the Church of Rome teacheth and practiseth doctrines destructive of salvation. Therefore the Church of Rome is to be relinquished.' See D'Oyly's 'Life,' vol. i., p. 176.

and godly love' (see 'Papers on Eucharistic Presence,' p. 375).

What would the learned Dr. William Clagett say? He was cut off in the prime of life, but not before he had won for himself a name and authority inferior to that of very few of his day. He is ranked by Bishop Burnet ('Own Time,' p. 307. London, 1857) among those who 'were indeed an honour, both to the Church and to the age in which they lived.' And thus he wrote, 'If the corruptions of the Roman Church (which God forbid) should ever come to be established in this Church of England again by the same authority that has abolished them, it were not only lawful, but a necessary duty to separate from the communion of this Church in that case' (Enchirid. Theol. Anti-R., pp. 692, 693). And again, 'We say that they who in Queen Mary's days chose to lay down their lives rather than return to the communion of the Roman Church, were so far from being schismatics, that they were God's martyrs in so doing' (*ibid.*, p. 694).

What would the estimable and learned Bishop George Hooper, the friend and successor of the saintly Bishop Ken,* say? This is what he did say: 'Who would not stand amazed to hear that Church styled popish, the purity of whose faith has been declared so expressly, so illustriously attested and spoken of through all the world? .... What a new wonder must this be to the world, to hear the Church constituted by Cranmer and Ridley accused of popery! the faith and worship suspected to be unreformed, which was delivered to us by those great martyrs! .... If this Church and these men, after the declaration made in our Articles, after repeated subscriptions and abrenunciations, after all this zealous opposition of popery, must yet be suspected of popery; as well, on the other side, may the decrees of Trent be said to comply with the Reformation, and the Pope himself be thought to be a Protestant. One would imagine, from the suspicions of these men that traduce us, that there was some small inconsiderable difference betwixt the papists and us, something that

---

* As to Ken's own views, see Dean Plumptre's 'Life of Ken,' vol. i., p. 236, and especially Goode on 'Eucharist,' ii., pp. 706-710 and 892-896. See also 'Eucharistic Presence,' pp. 155, 156.

might easily be reconciled; not that we differ as much from them, in all necessary points, as those very persons they pretend to follow. For let all the harmony of Protestant confessions be consulted, and see if we are not of the harmony, and our Articles do not conspire with theirs; if ours are not as express and as directly opposite to the Roman Church; if there can be any hopes of reconciling us sooner than of reconciling them' (Works, vol. i., pp. 3, 4. Oxford, 1855).

Assuredly such Churchmen as these would have had little sympathy with efforts to emasculate the Protestantism of our formularies, to stifle the witness of our Prayer-book against the errors of the Church of Rome, and to turn aside the arrow of our Articles' condemnation—aimed straight at the sacrifices of Masses—to strike only an obscure, an insignificant and preposterous delusion, in order that the sacrifice of the Mass may be again defended, upheld, and established. Surely we may venture to ask our friends who are in danger of being misled by specious arguments to pause and consider whither they are tending.

Are we prepared to stand up and charge our

great English divines with heresy? Are we ready to gird on new weapons of warfare and fight under an alien banner in defence of doctrines which they so strenuously opposed?

At least, let us first bring the controversy afresh into the light of God's truth, and see whether they were not right in insisting that the sacrifices of Masses were blasphemous fables and dangerous deceits.

To what shall we attribute the use of such plain speaking and such strong language as applied by these divines to the Church of Rome?

Doubtless, those who have been able to persuade themselves that the doctrine of the Mass is a true doctrine, and that our Article XXXI. has nothing to say concerning the teaching of Rome, may consistently set it down to the account of an unhappy persistence of the evil feeling engendered by what they regard as the heats and mistakes and hasty proceedings of the Reformation period. It is not to be wondered at if in the ears of such it has a sound as of 'bitterness and wrath, and anger and clamour, and evil speaking,' which should be put away from us with all malice.

But it cannot be so accounted for by those whose sacred convictions have led them to see in our Article XXXI. a faithful witness against something more serious than mediæval superstition, and are fully persuaded that the Church of Rome hath erred not only in their living and manner of ceremonies, but also in matters of faith.

If the teaching of our Article XXXI. is a true teaching, to stand clearly, in this matter, on the side of the Reformation is a solemn duty.

If the testimonies alleged in this compilation against the sacrifice of the Mass are not all and altogether founded on error, it is the part of Christian charity to bear true and faithful witness against the errors and corruptions of Rome, and to speak out in no doubtful language against specious invitations to re-union with a system which 'by consequent' is antagonistic to the simplicity of the Gospel.

Certainly such faithful witness is not to be attributed to any lack of true charity or true wisdom.

In a note on his essay on 'Union with Rome' the late Bishop C. Wordsworth of Lincoln wrote

(p. 74): 'Some most eminent for charity and wisdom, in the present age, have set the example of reviving the language of Hooker and Bishop Andrewes on this point. In a conversation which the author of this essay had with a prelate distinguished alike by learning and mildness, our late revered primate, Archbishop Howley, his grace adverted to this subject, and declared, as his own opinion, that " as long as the Seven Hills of Rome are standing, so long will it be clear to all who reflect, that the Church of Rome is the Babylon of St. John."'

In the same essay Bishop Wordsworth says: 'It has been shown in those vindications [of our own divines] that it is the bounden duty of all Churches to avoid strife, and to *seek peace, and ensue it.* But it was also demonstrated, no less clearly, that unity in *error* is *not true* unity, but is rather to be called a conspiracy against the God of unity and truth' (p. 78).

'Doubtless [he adds] there is a unity when everything in nature is wrapped in the gloom of night, and bound with the chains of sleep. Doubtless there is a unity when the earth is congealed by frost and mantled in a robe of snow. Doubtless there is a unity when the human voice is still, the hand motionless, the breath suspended, and the human frame is locked in the iron grasp of death. And doubtless there is a unity when men surrender their reason, and sacrifice their liberty, and stifle their conscience, and seal up Scripture, and deliver themselves captives, bound hand and foot, to the dominion of the Church of Rome. But this is not the unity of vigilance and light; it is the unity of sleep and gloom. It is not the unity of warmth and life; it is the unity of cold and death. It is not true unity, for it is not UNITY in the TRUTH' (pp. 78, 79).

A little further on, speaking of the Apocalypse, the bishop says: 'In this divine book the Spirit of God has portrayed the Church of Rome such as none but He could have foreseen she would become, and such as, wonderful and lamentable to say, she *has* become. He has thus broken her magic spells; He has taken the wand of enchantment from the hand of this spiritual Circe; He has lifted the mask from her face; and with His Divine finger He has written her true character in large letters, and has planted her title on her forehead, to be seen and read by all — " MYSTERY, BABYLON THE GREAT, THE MOTHER OF THE ABOMINATIONS OF THE EARTH " ' (pp. 81, 82).

Let me add from the same learned divine the following statement written at a time when he was drawing nearer to the close of this life : ' After a careful meditation for many years upon these prophecies concerning the Apocalyptic Babylon, the present writer here solemnly, in the presence of the Omniscient Searcher of hearts, who dictated these awful predictions, records this as his deliberate judgment upon them, probably for the last time ' (' Commentary on Rev. xvii.,' p. 246).

But in view of the testimonies against the Romish Mass doctrine which are here brought together, the question will probably be asked, What is the true value of any such collection ? Has not the very name of *catena* been brought into contempt by the facility with which theological writings may be cited (and too often have been cited) in support of views which the writers themselves never held ? And may not other quotations from English divines be multiplied to discredit the argument which these testimonies are alleged to support?

In answer to all such questions, those who would desire truly to study and examine the matter should be asked to see clearly a distinction which very really exists between ambiguous language cited in support of a positive doctrine and clear statements of the negation and rejection of any such doctrine.

Archbishop Longley, in his 'Posthumous Charge' (p. 29), well and truly said : 'A single disclaimer of a meaning which might be attributed to his language, a single explanation on his part of what might otherwise be doubtful, a single correction of a phrase which might otherwise mislead, surely serves as a general interpretation of an author's meaning in other passages where the like correction or explanation does not occur.'

A quotation may be made as in support of a doctrine commonly known by such or such a name—a name which in its ambiguities also admits another—a secondary sense. And the very context may show clearly that the writer is using the term *not* in the sense which it is alleged to defend. And the force of the quotation may obviously thus be utterly evacuated by simply showing that the writer repudiated the doctrine in support of which he was called as a witness.

We know what serious mistakes have thus been made through the ambiguity of the term 'real presence.'

But it is clearly quite otherwise with the unambiguous language by which a doctrine is clearly and distinctly rejected and negatived.

This distinction may easily be illustrated by applying it to the matter before us. It will be seen that there is a certain sense in which English divines have safely used the word '*offer*'; sometimes have defended the language which speaks of *offering Christ for the living and the dead*, yet with explanatory limitations which have made evident that the words are not to be understood in the ordinary sense in which they are used by Romish divines. (See below, Appendix B.)

But the language of these same English divines, in which they deny and repudiate the Romish doctrine of the Mass, can never be brought to nought by any special pleadings or specious arguments derived from the ambiguities of language.

The statements of doctrinal assertion may be often misunderstood. The statements of doctrinal negation are commonly unmistakable.

If the question be asked, Are there, then, no quotations which may fairly be made from English divines to support the Romish view of the Eucharistic Sacrifice? I answer that I know none. If I am in error I shall be thankful to be corrected, but I am not aware that any divine of esteem can be cited whose testimony can be fairly set to weigh in the opposite scale to that of the testimonies which are here collected.

In his explanatory letter to Dr. Jelf, published in the year 1841, Newman replied to the charge that Tract 90 asserted that the Thirty-nine Articles 'do not contain any condemnation of the doctrines of Purgatory, Pardons, Worshipping and Adoration of Images and Relics, the Invocation of Saints, and the Mass, as they are *taught authoritatively* in the Church of Rome, but only of certain absurd practices and opinions, which intelligent Romanists repudiate as much as we do;' and he declared, 'On the contrary, I consider that they *do* contain a condemnation of the authoritative teaching of the Church of Rome on these points; I only say that, whereas they were written before the decrees of Trent, they were not directed against those decrees' (p. 4).

Yet we have the assurance of Newman himself (given in the year 1879) that 'although the Ninetieth "Tract for the Times" did not even go so far as to advocate the *Sacerdotium* in the Catholic sense, but only the possibility of interpreting the Thirty-first Article in a sense short of its denial, Dr. Routh told the Bishop of Oxford, who consulted him on the point, that such interpretations generally as those advocated in the Tract were a *simple novelty* in Anglican history' (Preface to Hutton's 'Anglican Ministry,' p. xvi).

It will be readily admitted, I suppose, by all, that very few men indeed could speak on such a point with greater authority than Dr. Routh.

And his authority may well be appealed to in confirmation of the persuasion that no support will be found from any esteemed divine of the English Church for the Mass doctrine as now by some reintroduced among us. But let me not be misunderstood.

I do not mean that there are no testimonies of divines of the English Church, which, at first sight, might well appear to be in opposition to the testimonies which are here collected.

Bishop Forbes (of Edinburgh), in his 'Considerationes Modestæ,' manifests a most irenical tendency. Bishop Burnet says of him: 'I do not deny but his earnest desire of general peace and union among all Christians made him too favourable to many of the corruptions of the Church of Rome' (in Preface to 'Life of Bishop Bedell'). But it is clear that he deals with the minimized view of the Romish doctrine, and relies much on quotations from pre-Tridentine writers, whose views are not those of post-Tridentine Romanism. And he bears true witness against what goes beyond this. Moreover, he nowhere (I believe) aims at anything like evacuating the natural meaning of our Article XXXI. by applying it to any such doctrine as that attributed to Catharinus (see his Works, vol. ii., pp. 581-613, A.C.L.*).

It is true that quotations may be made from some English divines which, viewed in their isolation, might seem to make small account of the distinction—*quoad* sacrifice—between the theology of England and that of Rome. But this will be found to be the result of the inconsistencies of the Romish doctrine, and the tendency of Romish divines to present in controversy the minimized view of the sacrifice and propitiation to be dealt with by their opponents (see 'Romish Mass and English Church,' pp. 26-29, 44).

It was well for English divines to attempt *to hold* their adversaries to this view—and to say, 'We are with you so far as sacrificial remembrance and representation and application—and you can't go a step beyond this without blasphemy.' 'Speak *distinctly*, and we cannot tell what you desire more than we hold' (see

---

* As to the language of Andrewes and Laud, and Cosin and Bramhall, see 'The Theology of Bishop Andrewes,' pp. 17, 18, 25, 26; 'The Real Presence of the Laudian Theology,' pp. 49-52; 'Papers on the Eucharistic Presence,' pp. 538, 563.

Bramhall, as quoted below, pp. 153-155, and Works, vol. i., pp. 54, 55, A.C.L.).

But it would obviously be a mistake to suppose that, therefore, these English divines were blind to the fact that Romish doctrine did *not* 'speak distinctly,' and could not teach consistently such a view as alone could be defended, and did (in its other aspect—as seen from another side) go beyond the boundary into the region of blasphemous fables and dangerous deceits (see again Bramhall, as quoted below, pp. 153-155, and in 'Eucharistic Presence,' p. 538). How could it be otherwise, so long as the sacrifices of Masses were made to rest for their foundation on the real presence of transubstantiation, and their efficacy was made to depend, not merely on any remembrance or representation, but upon a real offering of Christ by the priest for the quick and the dead?

And so it should be observed that in dealing with Romish objections to our orders, bearing on the omission of the power of sacrificing, our divines of former generations (even those of Laudian tendencies) never pleaded in answer, 'We hold and teach as you do the sacrifice of the Mass, and claim for our priests the same power of offering Christ for the living and the dead; our objection is only to *abuses* of your doctrine.' But the position they maintained and defended was this: 'We, of the Church of England, acknowledge a representation, commemoration, application of the sacrifice of the Cross in the Eucharist.' 'And further than this you dare not go—cannot go without blasphemy' (see Bishop Cosin, as quoted below, pp. 162-166).

But it is certain that their opponents never consented to be content with this. Post-Tridentine theology too plainly refused to be restrained by any such limitations.

It was truly said by the non-juror Spinckes, 'This will not suffice, for the Council of Trent anathematizes such as proceed no further' ('Answer to Proposal for Catholic Communion,' p. 142. London, 1705. See 'Romish Mass and English Church,' pp. 28, 29).

If perhaps one or two of these English divines may seem to have entertained a thought of the possibility of explanatory concessions on the Romish side (in the better understanding of the subject on both sides; see Bramhall's Works, vol. ii., p. 582, A.C.L.) by which her doctrine might be made consistent, and her language speak distinctly according to the teaching of the Reformed (see Bramhall's Works, vol. i., pp. 80, 81, 279), it will never (I believe) be found that any one of these showed any disposition to deduct anything from the teaching of our Article as understood in its natural and obvious sense, and as applied to the Romish doctrine of Masses.

Probably the most doubtful case is that of Bishop Montague (see Prynne's 'Canterbury's Doom,' p. 352. London, 1646). But it must not be supposed that in Bishop Montague's projects for union (see Perry's 'History of the Church of England,' vol. i., p. 347) there was no difficulty felt as to points of doctrine, and especially as to the Eucharist (see Berington's 'Memoirs of Panzani,' pp. 238, 242). Other pacificators (in 'The Pope's Nuncios') insisted on some concessions in *doctrine*, 'otherwise no accord could be' (see 'Real Presence of Laudian Theology,' p. 54, note).

However unfavourable may be the impression of Montague's action conveyed by the history, it is fair to take our view of his doctrine from his own writings (see Hallam's 'Const. Hist.,' vol. ii., pp. 69-74, and Nicholls, 'Def. Eccl. Angl.,' p. 139.)

And little account may be taken of what he may have said to Panzani concerning the bishops (see Panzani's 'own report to the Pope,' as quoted by Hallam, p. 68, note). Hallam says (p. 70): 'It appears almost certain that Montague made too free with the name of the archbishop, and probably of many others; and it is well worthy of remark, that the popish party did not entertain any sanguine hopes of the King's conversion.'

It should be observed that Panzani had orders 'not to touch upon particulars, nor give encouragement that there should be any relaxation on the Catholic side, as to the *credenda* or fundamentals of religion' (see Berington's 'Memoirs of Panzani,' p. 242).

If it were so that Bishop Montague was at any time led on by his vanity (p. 241) into something like playing a double part (which we may be slow to believe till we have other evidence than that of Panzani's 'Memoirs,' p. 248), the character of others ought not to be compromised. But we are told, 'The truth is, Panzani was apprehensive, the bishop still entertained some opinions inconsistent with the fundamentals of the Roman Catholic religion' ('Memoirs,' p. 242). And it is clear that he had made himself responsible for such opinions on the Eucharistic Presence and the Mass Sacrifice (see 'Answer to Gag,' pp. 252, 263, 265, and 'Apello Cæsarem,' pp. 294, 287). And, indeed, it is very observable that among the opinions imputed to him by Pym's Committee as 'contrary to the book of homilies and the Thirty-nine Articles' (see Neale's 'History of Puritans,' vol. i., p. 507), there is not found any one pertaining to the doctrine of the Mass, or the teaching of Article XXXI.

It is unhappily not to be denied that Laud had tendencies which led him to take the most favourable view of Romish doctrine, a view far more favourable than that of the reformers. His natural temper, his surroundings, and the difficulties of his position, and his desire to win the English papists (see 'Cyprianus Anglicus,' p. 417), all tended to draw him towards an assimilation (in externals at least) to the Romish system. But this very fact, and the knowledge of the temptations which were set before him,* make it all the more evident that the sense of doctrinal differences made reconciliation with the Romish Church, in his view, impossible, without doctrinal† concessions on the side of Rome (see Heylyn's 'Cyprianus Anglicus,' pp. 414, 416, 419). We might gather this even from 'The Pope's Nuncios,' if we accepted as unquestionable all that is contained in that singular publication (see Goode's 'Rome's Tactics,' pp. 34, 35. Nisbet, 1893). And the testimony of Laud's writings undoubtedly suffices to make it evident that among these doctrinal differences Rome's teach-

* In his speech on the impeachment, Laud said: 'It cannot be imagined by any reasonable man, but that, if I could have complied with Rome, I should not have wanted either honour or profit' (Hook's 'Life of Laud,' p. 362). And he appeals to 'the number of those persons whom, by God's blessing upon my labours, I have settled in the true Protestant religion established in England' (*ibid.*, p. 363).

† It is, indeed, passing strange that Heylyn (who admits that 'no such reconcilation was upon the anvil'—'Cyprianus Anglicus,' p. 417) should have thought a reconciliation with Rome possible upon terms such as these: 'The bishops of England to be independent of the Popes of Rome; the clergy to be permitted the use of marriage; the people to receive the Communion in both kinds, and all divine offices officiated in the English tongue; NO INNOVATION MADE IN DOCTRINE' (p. 416).

ing concerning the Eucharist held a prominent place.* On this point the teaching of Laud, and of the Laudian school, misrepresented as it has been, is not open to the charge of unfaithfulness. I believe I have given good and sufficient evidence of this elsewhere (see 'The Real Presence of Laudian Theology,' especially p. 50). Here it must suffice to appeal to the quotations made from Laud's writings in the present compilation, and especially to the distinct assertion of his bosom friend, and devoted admirer, his *alter ego*, Peter Heylyn.

Whatever error Heylyn may have fallen into (and the reader is not asked to be an admirer of the man or his writings) he can hardly be charged with teaching anything like the Romish doctrine of the Mass. Witness the following: 'The Article ... determineth positively that the sacrifices of Masses, *in the which it was commonly said that the Priests did offer Christ for the*

---

* So Heylyn, 'next to the point of the supremacy, esteemed the principal Article of religion in the Church of Rome (" primus et præcipuus Romanensis fidei articulus ") as is affirmed in the " History of the Council of Trent," the most material differences betwixt them and us relate to the Sacrament of the Lord's Supper, and the natural efficacy of good works ' (' Cyprianus Anglicus,' p. 21).

quick and the dead, to have remission of pain or guilt, were blasphemous fables, and dangerous deceits. And therefore had the Vicar of Gr—— erected, or intended to erect, an altar for such a sacrifice, he had not only sacrificed his discretion on it, but also his religion, and been *no longer worthy to be called a son of the Church of England*' ('Coal from the Altar,' Sect. I., p. 7. London, 1636). See further quotations from Heylyn below, pp. 149-152.

At least, then, we should hesitate to lay a denial of the natural sense of our Article XXXI. to the charge of Laud or his followers. We may, some of us, have our dislikes and suspicions as regards many of Laud's doings and sayings. We may contrast unfavourably Laudian theology with the theology of the Reformation; but in justice we are bound not to accuse it of teaching the Romish doctrine of the Mass.

But I may reasonably be expected to make some special reference to No. 81 of 'Tracts for the Times.'

That tract contains a *catena* of 'Testimony of writers of the later English Church to the doctrine of the Eucharistic Sacrifice.' The date of this is November 1, 1837 (see Pusey's 'Life,' vol. iii., p. 479). At this date Pusey's view of the sacrifice (though differing doubtless from that of the Reformers) appears to have fallen far short of what is now maintained by some extreme teachers among us. He acknowledges that 'the *Church of Rome* had connected with the true doctrine' 'blasphemous fables and dangerous deceits' (p. 2); that '*her* doctrine of the sacrifice interfered with that of the one sacrifice on the Cross' (p. 4). He says, 'The Romish Church corrupted and marred the Apostolic doctrine in two ways: 1st, by the error of transubstantiation; 2nd, by that of purgatory. And in both there occurs that peculiar corruption of the administrators of the Romish Church, that they countenance so much more of profitable error than in their abstract system they acknowledge' (p. 7). He speaks of 'the Romish error, "that Christ was offered for the quick and dead"' (p. 11), and of 'the false doctrine,' that 'in the Mass, the priest did offer Christ for the quick and dead' (p. 13).

It is, therefore, not to be wondered at that the authorities quoted give no support to the Romish doctrine, and make no attempt to explain away the natural meaning of our Article XXXI., though some of them show a disposition to minimize the errors of Rome. They do not maintain any hypostatical oblation of Christ. Those who speak of the offering of the body and blood of Christ, give us to understand that the offering is to be understood as in mystery, or representation, or commemoration. And though some use the word 'propitiatory,' it is in the secondary sense, which is separated by a wide gulf indeed from its primary and stricter sense, or, to use the words of Pusey, ' in no other sense than Cranmer calls "gratificatory" . . . *i.e.*, such a sacrifice as doth not reconcile us to God, but is made of them as be reconciled ' (p. 51), or which Waterland calls 'propitiatory in a sober qualified sense'* (p. 52; see especially Works, vol. v.,

---

* We need hardly wonder at what is related concerning I. Casaubon by Barclay: '"Nihil," inquit Casaubonus, "opus est ut labores; sponte profiteor, et ex Ecclesiæ antiquæ ritibus constare contendo, Eucharistian esse sacrificium: Nec sacrificium modo laudis, ut plurimi nostri volunt, sed sacrificium propitiatorium, sacrificium ἱλαστικόν." Hæc ipsius verba fuere.' On this his son replies: 'Multa possent responderi (ne de Barclaii fide dubitem) ex Patrum sententiâ, quæ non sunt hujus loci' (quoted from Forbes, 'Considerationes Modestæ,' vol. ii., p. 602, A.C.L.). His

p. 281), 'in which large acceptation (*i.e.*, after a large and improper manner of speech'), says Bishop Morton, 'Protestants may account it 'propitiatory also' (p. 93. See Cranmer 'On Lord's Supper,' p. 361.)

One of these writers (H. Thorndike), whose incautious language it is sometimes difficult to uphold or defend, regards 'the profession of Christianity' to be propitiatory (p. 172); and of the language of Rome, 'Quod in Missa Christus incruente immolatur,' he says, 'If it be meant properly, it is a contradiction; for that which hath blood is not sacrificed but by the shedding of the blood of it; if figuratively, it signifies no more than that which I have said, that it is represented, commemorated, and offered as slain' (p. 180).

Another (Dr. G. Hickes, following the writer

---

language may well be understood in the sense of Amandus Polanus, 'Propitiatorium vero aliquo modo, quatenus unici illius sacrificii vere propitiatorii memoriam in eo serio frequentare jubemur, quod Filius Dei a Patre Missus ipse in propriâ personâ semel pro nobis obtulit' (*ibid.*, p. 604).

That Casaubon did not use the word in the Romish sense may be fairly argued from the following: 'Aliquando Eucharistia appellatur τὸ δῶρον, eandem ob causam, propter quam dicitur et sacrificium; quia videlicet est commemoratio sacrificii semel a Christo oblati' ('Exercitationes ad Annales Eccles. Baronii,' xvi., § li., p. 576. London, 1614).

mistaken for Overall—see p. 74), says of prayer, 'That is propitiatory too' (see 'Papers on Eucharistic Presence,' p. 538); and elsewhere he says: 'The ancient notion of this holy sacrament being a commemorative sacrifice, in which we represent before God the sacrifice of Christ upon the Cross, perfectly secures the holy mystery from that corrupt and absurd notion [*i.e.*, "the popish notion of it"], it being impossible that a solemn commemoration of a fact or thing should be the fact or thing itself' (quoted in Tract 81, p. 274).

Another (following the example of St. Augustin — see Waterland's Works, vol. v., p. 283) speaks of each Christian as in baptism 'offering the sacrifice of Christ's Passion for his sins' (*ibid.*, p. 86).

Another, whose views were regarded as very eccentric and extreme, the author of 'The Unbloody Sacrifice,' separated his own sacrificial doctrine most clearly and distinctly from what he regarded as 'so abominable corruption' as 'the sacrifice of the Mass' (see Tract 81, p. 310, and 'The Eucharist considered in its Sacrificial Aspect,' p. 10), and contended that the consecrated elements 'may therefore be called a sacrifice, as a representation may justly be called by the name of its principal' (quoted in Tract 81, p. 313).

The doctrine for which the most extreme of these erratic writers (many of them nonjurors) contended may be fairly expressed in the words of Brett, 'That our Blessed Saviour did leave His own supper as a commemorative, eucharistical, material sacrifice, a sacrifice of impetration, as well as gratulatory, showing forth our Saviour's death, presenting it before God as our all-sufficient propitiation, and as being an especial means of obtaining the benefits of it for us; and, in a word, that it is propitiatory' (Tract 81, p. 384).

We may think the language of some of these writers likely to lead to much confusion of thought, and capable of leading to serious error of belief. We may question some of their statements. We may dispute some of their arguments. We may think that Waterland did well to oppose what was novel and peculiar in some of their doctrines. We may condemn with him their 'unwarrantable excesses' (Works, vol. v., p. 145). We may differ from them, as we may think they differed from the more Scriptural teaching of our earlier theology (see Van Mildert in Waterland's Works, vol. i., pp. 204-210. Oxford, 1843). Some among us may, perhaps, feel strongly that there was a dangerous mistake in their teaching. But in fairness it must be acknowledged that their doctrine stands separate by a great and impassable gulf from the Romish doctrine of the Mass, a doctrine which they were as ready to repudiate and condemn as any of our divines who had gone before them.

Indeed, Father Davenport (after his laboured endeavour to explain away the sense of our Article) wrote, in 1655, 'Even they who are most temperate unanimously deny *Sacerdotem offerre Christum*, which destroys the very life of our Christian sacrifice' (see Hutton's 'Anglican Ministry,' p. 370).

And Smith, in his 'Epistolary Dissertation,' says truly (see Lathbury's 'History of Non-jurors,' p. 379), 'Our doctrine of the sacrifice was, in the dispute between the late Dr. Hickes and his opponents, formerly cried down as popish. Of this imputation Dr. Waterland has been so just as to clear it, for which we cannot but return him our thanks; because it is evident it is entirely inconsistent with the popish, and overthrows it, there being as much difference between it and the Romish as between the substance of bread and wine, and the substance of our Blessed Saviour's body and blood.'

As regards the teaching of Tract 81, it was said by Dean Goode, 'The writer of this Tract (if at least he is as learned as the professions of the Tractators would lead us to suppose) must have been perfectly aware that many of the authors whom he has here quoted would have utterly repudiated and reprobated the views of which he here quotes them as supporters' ('Divine Rule,' vol. ii., p. 355).

But I think it may be questioned whether, in passing so severe a censure, Dean Goode was fully taking into account the uncertainties of the writer's own doctrinal position at that date, and the limitations with which he seems to have surrounded its ambiguities.*

His doctrine is clearly separated from the Romish Mass doctrine, against which his statements are strong and severe. Witness the fol-

---

* Since writing the above, I find that Newman, in his 'Via Media,' speaking of Dr. Pusey's teaching in this Tract, declares, 'His antagonism in it to the Catholic dogma is unequivocal (vol. ii., p. 352).

lowing: 'When it was believed that Christ was "truly and indeed, in respect of His very body and blood, offered up to the Father under the form of bread and wine, in the daily sacrifice of the Church," nothing else, however abstractedly it might be allowed to be of use, could in comparison be of any moment. The corruptions, occasions of avarice, superstition, and profaneness, thence ensuing, exceeded all bounds' (pp. 8, 9).

Again: 'With Courayer's endeavours to extricate himself and his Church from the decrees of the Council of Trent, which fixed this language, we have nothing to do; certainly, the language of the Council on the sacrifice is in itself capable of a good interpretation, were it not that terms employed in it must be explained with reference to that Church's acknowledged doctrine of transubstantiation and purgatory. And THE DOCTRINE OF THE SACRIFICE CANNOT BE THE SAME, WHERE TRANSUBSTANTIATION IS HELD AND WHERE IT IS NOT.... If "true and proper" means "physical, corporeal, substantial,' *i.e.*, implies "transubstantiation," we reject it' (pp. 46, 47).

Again: 'These writers' [Courayer and Nicole] 'make the sacrifice both the same (as that on the

Cross) and distinct; through transubstantiation the same, and yet, in act, distinct' (p. 8).

But, while a doubt may be felt as to the doctrine which Dr. Pusey was then advocating, there can hardly be a question that the authors quoted in the Tract would have utterly rejected the Mass doctrine as now taught by some among us.

For further important evidence of this subject the reader may be referred to a note on 'Eucharistic Doctrine of the Non-juring School,' in Bishop Dowden's 'Historical Account of the Scottish Communion Office,' pp. 329-338.

In conclusion, I will only venture to say that while I cannot doubt that in these days controversy on this important subject is a duty, I trust that on both sides of the controversy those who are called to engage in it may earnestly desire, and endeavour, and pray that they may be ever, in the sight of God, ἀληθεύοντες ἐν ἀγάπῃ.

May God's Holy Spirit of truth guide us into the whole truth as it is in Jesus, and reveal to our admiring and adoring hearts the full truth, in its exceeding blessedness and saving power, of His one, full, perfect, and sufficient sacrifice, oblation, and satisfaction for the sins of the whole world!

SUPPLEMENTAL POSTSCRIPT.

But, after all, it is impossible not to recognise the fact—and indeed to some extent it may be recognised with thankfulness—that there is something in the tendency and temper of our times which can hardly fail to blunt the edge of any argument from the traditional teaching of a National Church.

Thoughts such as these will doubtless find avenues of influence, if not of expression : 'These are days when men feel the galling of traditional chains, and are obliged to turn a blind eye upon confessions of faith. And it is an anachronism to expect that much weight will be given to the testimonies of fallible men, who, in former days, have doubtless been well content to follow the lead of those who had gone before them, and who, in their turn, had been blindly led by inherited prejudices. Some allowance must be made for our living in days quite different from those which these writers represent. Men's thoughts are no longer to be restrained by tradition, and men's faith should be set free from the binding of Articles of Religion. Other sciences are using their liberty to make wonderful advances. Why should not theology also be free to go forward ?'

We may be very loath to strain tight what equity and charity may incline us (as far as may be) to make elastic. But we must ask—Will such pleadings as these avail to discharge the securities which (in defence of what she regards as God's truth on a most important subject) the Church of England has thought right to take of those whom she admits to minister in her courts ? Will they be able to countervail the fact of Articles subscribed, of doctrines accepted as the teaching of the Church of England, of doctrines rejected as (by a general consensus of our divines) the dangerous deceits of the Church of Rome ?

I can hardly believe that it will be so with those, who—however they may value the progress of theological science, and desire its advance

—have been taught to know that the one faith, once for all delivered to the saints, is unchanging as its Divine Author, 'Jesus Christ, the same yesterday, and to-day and for ever,' always the same saving and enlightening truth, which is hid from the wise and prudent, and revealed unto babes.

In truth, it is no light matter to presume upon the confidences which belong to the traditions of any society whatever.

Much more is it a very serious matter to violate the trusts which belong to the sacred traditions—recognised and accepted as such—of a great National Church, and a mother of Churches.

All doubtless are agreed that to decline to accept anything *merely* because our fathers before us believed it is right. A poor and miserable thing, indeed, is the Churchmanship of a merely traditional Christianity. The faith of the Christian Church rests not on the word of man, but on the word of God; and it is taught to human hearts not by the tradition of men, but by the power of God.

But all will probably be agreed also in this— that human tradition has its place in the divine economy of Revelation; and that to refuse assent to anything because it was the faith of our ancestors is certainly wrong.

We must, of course, decline to accept as the major premiss for faith's syllogism, 'All that comes to us recommended by authority and tradition must needs be true.' Our own responsibilities may not thus be put aside.

But we may surely be right, and not wrong, in looking at the faith of our forefathers with a presumption rather in favour of its truth than with a settled prejudice against it.

And assuredly we cannot give ourselves to the ministry of the one faith as received in the Reformed Church of England, if, in defiance of the traditional teaching of all her eminent divines, we can only say our 'Yea' to a teaching—the teaching of a *dangerous deceit*—to which she solemnly charges us to say 'Nay.'

The tendency to ignore and discredit traditional beliefs has indeed shown itself abundantly among neologians, not only in England, but in America also, and on the Continent of Europe.

But this impatience of all control and guidance from inherited types of religious teaching is not to be looked upon as peculiar to a rationalistic school of thought.

Dr. Pusey appears to have regarded the 'Catholic' interpretation of our Articles as that which alone brought out their natural sense, and the Protestant sense as simply the result of a mistaken but persistent tradition. Thus he wrote in 1866: 'We had all been educated in a traditional system which had practically imported into the Articles a good many principles which were not contained in them nor suggested by them, yet which were habitually identified with them' (Revised Preface to reprint of Tract 90, p. v.). And again: 'We proposed no system to ourselves, but laid aside, piece by piece, the system of ultra-Protestant interpretation, which had encrusted round the Articles' (p. vi.). And again: 'I vindicated it [Tract 90] in my letter to Dr. Jelf as the *natural* grammatical interpretation of the Articles' ('Eirenicon,' p. 31).

It is no wonder, then, that the so-called Catholic school should be found fretting under the teaching of what, in their view, is a traditional misunderstanding and an inherited misrepresentation of the teaching of our Articles.

If they are right in their view that their sense is the *natural* sense, they do well to be in rebellion against the traditional perversions of that sense.

But *are* they right? Have we not rather here an example of that which has too often shown itself in the history of the Christian Church—a presuming on the power of dialectical subtleties, and the authority of theological learning to put out the eyes of common-sense?

Surely the history of the English Reformation has something to say on this matter.*

Can we be quite wrong in thinking that the fires around the stakes to which our martyred forefathers were bound are casting a lurid light

---

* Bishop Bull says ('Vindication of the Church of England,' xxv.) our Thirty-nine Articles are *mainly directed* against 'the errors and corruptions of the Church of Rome.' Does anyone question the historical truth of this assertion? Yet, because some who have subscribed the Articles have come to think and feel very differently of Romish doctrine, therefore now, *first*, the Articles are made to pass through a cruel rack of torture, out of which it is hoped their sense may come so crushed and flexible as easily to adapt themselves to a position of substantial agreement with Rome: and *then*, because certain hard joints are found too firm to yield to the severest pressure and the most ingenious devices of this unnatural process, therefore our Articles are condemned, and threatened with utter destruction.

on the only true and natural sense of our English Articles? (see 'Dangerous Deceits,' pp. 43-50).

Nay. Can we not make appeal to utterances even of Anglican 'Catholic' writers themselves, testifying that the 'Catholic' sense is certainly not the natural sense of our Articles of Religion?

An article in the 'Christian Remembrancer, of 1866, declares it 'impossible to deny that they (*i.e.* the Thirty-nine Articles) contain statements or implications that are verbally false, and others that are very difficult to reconcile with truth.' It ventures therefore to go a step beyond any suggestion in Dr. Pusey's 'Eirenicon,' and boldly proclaims its opinion, that before union with Rome can be effected, the Articles must be wholly withdrawn* (January, 1866, p. 188 ; see also p. 168).

* Who can wonder at the words of one who has separated himself from the influence of such teaching? 'Not one,' he says, ' of us but must own it ; not one but has writhed under the torture of doubting, whether on the threshold of this system, which he embraces to make him holy, there rests not the stain and semblance of a lie. Is this too harsh a term?' And again, 'Wonderful sophistry! Most solid ground of faith! Excellent school for guilelessness and sincerity! admirable preparation for making men holy, and good, and saintly, and everything that is Christian! except

Surely the very novelty* of the claim for such a 'Catholic' interpretation to be accepted as perhaps making them true!' ('Morality of Tractarianism,' pp. 8, 19). I have hesitated to transcribe such hard words. They are not mine. But as applied to *the system*, how are they to be gainsaid?

We may regret, but we can hardly wonder, that Archbishop Whateley should have spoken of Tract 90 as 'an example of hair-splitting and wire-drawing, of shuffling equivocations and dishonest garbling of quotations' ('Cautions for the Times,' p. 351).

We may regret, but we cannot condemn, such words of indignation as these: 'The more the matter is inquired into the more will the public mind perceive the disingenuousness and Jesuitism that have characterized the Tractarian movement' (Dean Goode's 'Tract 90 Historically Refuted.' See Saville's 'Dr. Pusey,' p. 60).

It was well said by Bishop Phillpotts of Exeter: 'As this [Tract 90] is by far the most daring attempt ever yet made by a minister of the Church of England to neutralize the distinctive doctrines of our Church, and to make us symbolize with Rome, I shall be excused if I detain you for a few minutes in unravelling the web of sophistry which has been laboriously woven to cover it. It rests mainly . . . on the allegation that the Articles were of a date anterior to the Decrees of Trent—an allegation having just that measure of truth which will enable it most effectually to deceive' ('Letters to Butler,' p. 319; see 'Dangerous Deceits,' pp. 60-71).

These are strong words, no doubt. But let it be noted that the Bishop says further on: 'I have done with the Tract. Let me only add, that I wish and hope that the intention of the writer, as declared by himself, may protect him from the severity of censure which the Tract itself deserves' (p 321).

* Though Sancta Clara hoped that by looking through his glasses Romanists might see Article XXXI, 'non adeo the natural sense is its own sufficient condemnation.

Who will be persuaded to believe that the natural sense of our Articles was unheard of and unknown for three centuries, and then brought to light by one who never claimed for it to be the *natural* sense, and who not long after became convinced of his untenable position, and seceded to

veritati discordem,' yet he did not maintain that the sense he gave to it was the true and *natural* sense. On the contrary, he begins by saying, 'Totus hic articulus durissimus videtur.' And in his 'Enchiridion of Faith,' published in 1655, he speaks of the English as denying the power of sacrificing the true body of Christ, and declaring such sacrifice a *pernicious imposture*. And he regards the doctrine even of the Laudian divines as destroying the very life of the Christian sacrifice (see Hutton's 'Anglican Ministry,' pp. 369, 370).

It is well to observe how the influence of Tract 90 is regarded in 'Catholic' circles. 'What could not be put out then [Tract No. 90] without a storm of abuse following is received now with acquiescence by one party, and with admiration by another; whilst the third great party into which we are divided is too feeble to put out any united efforts to destroy what it abominates' ('Christian Remembrancer,' January, 1866, p. 164). 'The principle of Protestantism is extinguished. That of Catholicism is triumphant' (*ibid.*, p. 167). 'The Church of England has made wonderful strides in the direction of Catholicism during the last twenty-five years. The acceptance of the Catholic interpretation of the Articles is the chief preliminary step' (*ibid.*, p. 168). Since this was written what advances have been made! And what wisdom displayed in the progress!

the communion of the Church against whose errors the teaching of our Articles was mainly directed.*

I find it then very hard to believe that there is really any question as to the *natural* meaning of our Article XXXI. But if a question must be made of it, I venture to think that the testimonies alleged in this book must have something material, something important, and something conclusive to say on that question.

I am not desiring to add anything from tradition to its natural sense. I am but appealing to tradition to bear witness against an unnatural attempt to spoil it of its only natural sense, and

---

* And it should be observed that, after his secession from the Church of England, Newman saw clearly how untenable had been his position as regards the interpretation of Article XXXI. In 'Via Media' (Longmans, 1891) he wrote: 'There is no denying then that these audacious words ["blasphemous fables and dangerous deceits"] apply to the doctrinal teaching as well as to the popular belief of Catholics. What was "commonly said" was also formally enunciated by the Œcumenical Hierarchy in Council assembled' (p. 352). Again: 'What then the Thirty-first Article repudiates is undeniably the central and most sacred doctrine of the Catholic religion; and so its wording has ever been read since it was drawn up' (*ibid.*).

It may seem strange, therefore, that in 1865 Newman should have written to Dr. Pusey, 'You are now republishing it (Tract 90) with my *cordial concurrence*' (see Holland's 'Cardinal Newman,' p. 12).

to leave in its utterance little more than the needless and uncalled for repetition of a truth which had already been distinctly affirmed in an earlier Article (Article II.).

But, further, I venture to ask that the value of these testimonies should be estimated mainly in view of what seems by some to be regarded as a very important discovery of the close of the nineteenth century as bearing on the interpretation of our Thirty-first Article. That Article, we are now asked to believe, was aimed only at some such monstrous corruption of the Mass-doctrine as was spoken of by some as 'the error of Thomas,' and denounced by others as 'the *deliratio* of Catharinus'—a heresy which Rome would be as ready to reject as any of the Reformers—a notion which was never really maintained by Albertus or Aquinas or Catharinus, though deriving some support from some misleading language in their works (see 'Dangerous Deceits,' Appendix, notes D, E, and G).

Now, I ask,—Is it likely, is it conceivable, that this could be so, and the whole succession of our divines, from the Reformation downwards, be utterly ignorant of it? Is it likely—is it possible, that this should be so, and our divines (and divines of the Church of Rome also) continually testifying to our rejection of the doctrine, not of Catharinus, but of Rome?

Here, then, I venture to think, is (for the time present) one chief value of these testimonies. I do not desire to over-estimate their importance as the opinions of individual men, however learned, and pious, and highly esteemed in their generations. But I believe their united witness to the real matter in controversy is fatal to the interpretation of the Article which has recently been commended to us.

So far as it is allowed that these testimonies give good witness to the tradition of the English Church, I believe it must be allowed that they close the door against the novel theory of a simply anti-Catharine aim in the teaching of our Article.

Let me be allowed to ask some special attention to this point. As it seems to me, it may not be lightly passed over.

It is surely an important fact to be observed that the doctrine of this Article was the subject of continual controversies between the learned divines of England and of Rome in the sixteenth and seventeenth centuries; and that (so far at least as I am aware) on neither side of the controversy was the Article ever supposed to be at all alluding to the alleged doctrine of Albertus or 'the error of Thomas,' or 'the madness of Catharinus.' On neither side was it ever (I believe) even questioned that the matter in dispute between the Churches was the very doctrine of the Mass itself, and nothing else. And even those writers on the Romish side, who, for reasons of their own, were anxious to make an easy pathway (or a pathway as easy as might be) from our side to theirs, and therefore to strain the language of our Articles into something like forced conformity with their own doctrines, never (I believe) ventured to explain away the sense of our Thirty-first Article by maintaining or suggesting that its condemnation was intended for the very peculiar and pernicious error attributed to the Archbishop of Conza.

Sancta Clara (C. Davenport), indeed, would get over the difficulty by supposing that the Article may be understood, *sobrie*, as levelled against a commonly received opinion ('Contra vulgarem et vulgatam opinionem,' p. 74. Edit. Lee) of a sacrificial efficacy *independent* of the sacrifice of the Cross ('independenter a Crucis sacrificio,' p. 74). And he maintains (ob hunc Articulum) that the sacrifice of the Cross is propitiatory *primo*, the sacrifice of the Mass *secundo* ('licet bene per se, et quasi secundo,' p. 75).*

* It must be observed that by a singular mistake (doubtless a misprint) Dr. F. G. Lee's translation, 'It must *not* be said that this sacrifice is of itself propitiatory' (p. 76), is the distinct negation of Sancta Clara's Latin, 'Dicendum tamen (ut dixi) esse etiam per se propitiatorium.' The difference is most important. (See below, Appendix, note B.) Sancta Clara goes on to argue that this must be allowed by our divines 'Cum enim ipsi fateantur in Ecclesiâ esse Sacerdotes, esse etiam sacrificia propitiatoria, fateantur necesse est. Nam ad Hebr. v.: *Omnis sacerdos constituitur, ut offerat dona et sacrificia pro peccatis.*' And thus he thinks to reconcile our Article with 'the sacrifice of Masses'! But where is the distinction between the *primo* and *secundo* in our Article? And where is the room to be found for the sacrifice which is '*propitiatorium secundo*,' and 'etiam per se propitiatorium'?

Laud declared in his defence, 'Some friends of his [Sancta Clara] brought him to me. His suit then was that he might print that book ["Deus, Natura, Gratia"] here. Upon speech with him I found the scope of his book to be such as that the Church of England would have little cause to thank him for it: and so absolutely denied it' (Laud's Works, vol. iv., p. 326, A.C.L.)

Davenport's book 'was much talked against by the Jesuits, who by all means would have it burnt, but being soon after licensed in Rome, gave a stop to any farther rumour of it. . . . In a letter also from Mr. Middleton (then chaplain to

It must be asked, in view of this assertion of this notion (this *vulgata opinio*) of an *independent* sacrificial efficacy of the Mass,—Was such an opinion ever prevalent? Was it upheld by the teaching of divines?

We may be sure Bishop Thirlwall did not speak hastily or unadvisedly when he said: 'To view the Mass as independent of the sacrifice of the Cross would indeed be a very gross error; but until I see some proof, I shall continue utterly to disbelieve that it is one into which any worshipper at the Mass, even in the darkest ages, ever fell. But though not independent of, it might be viewed as distinct from, the sacrifice of the Cross; and *so it is* viewed, not by the ignorant and vulgar only, but by the Church of Rome' (Charge of 1866, p. 140).

Yet it may, perhaps, be argued fairly, that to

Basil Lord Fielding, ambassador) to Archbishop Laud, dated at Venice in December, 1635, I find these passages, that the book of S. Clara relished not well with the Catholics, and that there was a consultation about it, and some did *extrema suadere*, and cried *ad ignem*. Father Tho. Talbot, a Jesuit of Paris, told him so by letter, who, talking with the Pope's nuncio at Paris about it, he told him 'twas the best course to let it die of itself, to which the nuncio, a moderate man, was inclinable' (Wood's 'Athenæ Oxonienses,' vol. iii., c. 1224. Edit. Bliss).

view the sacrifice as distinct might lead so naturally to the view of the Mass as independent,* that it is scarcely likely that among 'the ignorant and the vulgar' no 'worshipper at the Mass' was ever in danger of falling into some such error, or some such like misconceptions.

It can hardly be doubted that the tendency of much in the teaching of the monks was to lead the unlearned to look much rather to what the priest could now do for them in *his* sacrifice on the altar, than to what Christ had once done for them in *His* sacrifice on the Cross.†

---

* In Tract 90 Newman, shielding the Church of Rome from the aim of our Article, says: 'It is conceived then that the Article before us neither speaks against the Mass in itself, nor against its being an offering for the quick and the dead for the remission of sin; but against its being viewed ... as independent of, or distinct *from*, the sacrifice on the Cross, which is blasphemy' ('Via Media,' vol. ii., p. 326). This shows how at that date Newman himself could hardly have distinguished clearly between *independence* and *distinction*, and further that he must then have supposed that according to the doctrine of Rome, the oblation of the Mass was *not distinct* from the sacrifice of the Cross. For evidence of the *distinction*, according to the teaching of Romish divines, see 'Dangerous Deceits,' Appendix, Note A.

Bishop Thirlwall has given evidence from the Council of Trent, and the Romish Missal in his Charge of 1866, pp. 141-143.

† Bishop Thirlwall well says (p. 141): 'The sacrifice of the Mass might not the less practically supersede that of

And if only the view of the relation of the one sacrifice to the other were dim, or hazy, or latent (as it was surely not very unlikely to have been sometimes), then, I ask—Would it have been a very unnatural result if practically the sacrifice of the Mass were regarded as independent?

It is a matter on which we must expect to be guided mainly by arguments of probability.

But perhaps the opinion may be ventured without presumption, that what little help we have from occasional and dim sidelights of history seems rather to confirm the probability that in the darkness of ignorant times there may have been those in the lower grades of darkness and ignorance who had little apprehension of the teaching (though the very canon of the Mass should have taught it) that all the efficacy of the sacrifice of the altar was derived from the sacrifice of the Cross.

But this is an inquiry, the determination of which is of no great importance, because no one,

---

the Cross, if conceived as " distinct from," though not " independent of," this. And it is so conceived, not by the vulgar only, but by the Church of Rome, speaking through her most accredited doctors, and in her most sacred formularies.'

it may be supposed, will think of contending that our Articles were intended to concern themselves with such possible misconceptions of doctrine as might find place in the gross superstitions prevailing in the lowest depths of degraded ignorance. And as regards the better instructed classes there is no question to be made of the correctness of the Bishop's conclusion.

Among the more intelligent portion of the population there is very good evidence for the assurance that the notion of a really *independent* efficacy in the sacrifice of the Mass would have been regarded as inconsistent with the belief of the first elements of Christianity (see 'Dangerous Deceits,' pp. 27-39). And the idea of the sacrifice of the Cross being a satisfaction for original sin, while the sacrifice of the Mass was ordained for the taking away of actual sin, was an error the imputation of which was regarded as an insult to the educated mind of Christendom (*ibid.*, p. 36).

But the more important question is this,—Was such an opinion ever distinctly and consistently maintained by mediæval or Romish divines of any repute? Till more conclusive evidence is found than has yet been adduced, this may indeed be very well doubted. I believe it has been shown in 'Dangerous Deceits' that such an opinion cannot fairly be set down to the account of Albertus, or Aquinas, or Catharinus. Certainly the scholastics, as a rule, knew nothing of it (see 'Romish Mass and Eng. Ch.,' pp. 50-54). But probably the most questionable language on the subject may be found in the writings of Salmeron the Jesuit. His words are indeed sufficiently startling: 'Sola tamen actio quâ se obtulit in cœna, et quâ se obtulit in cruce, non tantum est oblatio, sed etiam sacrificium . . . et ita *sacrificium cœnæ non accipit ab illo crucis.* Deinde utraque oblatio in cœnâ, et in cruce ex eadem radice, *i.e.*, charitate et personâ Verbi vim atque efficaciam habent. Illud cœnæ infiniti valoris fuit, et unum infinitum non est majus alio.'

And it is, perhaps, even more surprising to read the words he has set in the margin as the summary of this teaching: 'Simplici ratione planum fit Christi oblationem in cœnâ nequaquam ab oblatione in cruce factâ vim suam et potestatem mutuari' ('Comment. in Evangel.

Hist.,' Tom. ix., Tract. 31, p. 247. Colon. Agrip., 1612).

It is not for me to attempt an explanation of this language. It is sufficient for my purpose to observe that in this very same chapter Salmeron insists on the derivative character of the Mass-sacrifice.*

---

* Compare the following from Aliphanus, spoken in the Council of Trent : ' Christus obtulit se in cœnâ expiatorie et propitiatorie, et ejusdem virtutis fuit illud sacrificium ac illud crucis . . . non minus fuit expiatoria oblatio cœnæ, quam crucis . . . et illud Christi sacrificium non habuit efficaciam a cruce ; sed a seipso, cum Christus de per se efficax sit, sicut et sacramentum in missâ ex se efficaciam habet, quia et ibi Christus, sed nisi oblatio Crucis facta fuisset, non potuisset nobis applicari' (see Theiner, ' Acta Conc. Trid.,' Tom. ii., pp. 93, 94). And the following from Leriensis : ' Necesse est dicere, quod verum sacrificium obtulerit et fuit propitiatorium per modum hostiæ oblatæ in cruce. . . . Non autem dicunt, quod unum sit expiatorium, et aliud non. . . . Et nostrum sacrificium habet efficaciam in virtute præteriti Christi sacrificii ' (*ibid.*, p. 84).

It should be remembered that when the minds of those in the Council were intensely exercised on the question whether or not it should be asserted that in His supper Christ offered Himself in sacrifice to God, and when it appeared that the Fathers and divines were nearly equally divided, it was Salmeron who made himself conspicuous by his earnestness in pressing for the affirmation. He occupied the whole space of one congregation with his own speech (see Mendham's ' Memoirs,' p. 226). We are told by Sarpi that ' Father Salmeron was the principal man to persuade the affirmative. He went to the houses of those men who

To me the teaching of Salmeron appears remarkably to illustrate the inconsistencies of the Romish Mass-doctrine. Certainly his words cannot fairly be alleged as evidencing that he distinctly and consistently taught that the efficacy of the Mass-sacrifice was independent of the sacrifice of the Cross. And I question whether any Romish divines now will be found to maintain that Salmeron meant to teach a doctrine so alien from the authoritative teaching of the Romish Church.

But even if he had, his teaching could certainly not have been identified with the error we have in view. The so-called 'Error of Thomas,' if indeed it involved the independence of the Mass (which may well be accounted as doubtful), certainly went far beyond it. The doctrine so-

were of the other opinion, especially those who had not given their voices, persuading them to be silent, or, at the least, to speak remissly' ('History of Council of Trent,' pp. 518, 519; Brett's translation).

It is much to be observed, however, that in the doctrine decreed the word 'propitiation' (as applied to the last supper) was designedly omitted, while (as applied to the Mass) it was distinctly asserted. So that now the Church of Rome teaches clearly that the priest does more than she has dared to say that Christ did (see 'Romish Mass and English Church,' p. 7).

called of Catharinus had its own peculiar features, of which not a trace is to be seen in the daring language of Salmeron.

I will make bold, then, to ask those who would now have us read this Ante-Catharine sense into the Article, whether they can produce any one saying from any one of the writings of anyone among the divines of any authority, on either side of the controversy, which can fairly be said to give any solid support to their view, or bear witness to the fact of such a restraint of the sense of the Article having been regarded as admissible in the century to which the language of the Article belongs?

Let such be humbly requested to look into this matter carefully for themselves, and see whether their present contention be not indeed but an after-thought of yesterday, conceived, as a last resort, to look something like a fair defence of a position which is really untenable and indefensible.

And if it be so that their sense of the Article is a novelty, and an unnatural novelty—a novelty necessitated by the teaching of a new doctrine, the doctrine of a new school of a new theology among us—a novelty alien from, and distinctly opposed to, the teaching of the Reformed Church of England—then may not the question well be asked—Can it be fair—can it be right for our new teachers to take an Article of the Church of England which was set up as a bulwark of oak and a strong fence firmly staked to exclude for ever the teaching of a certain doctrine of Rome, and out of it to make a plank, sawn out of it in their own mill, and fitted with their own tools (not of English manufacture), by which to slide in again among us that very doctrine which the Church of England certainly meant by this Article to teach us was a thing to be shut out, to be repudiated by all faithful men and rejected with holy indignation, as nothing less than a blasphemous fable and a dangerous deceit?*

* The authors of 'De Hierarchia Anglicanâ' would apparently have us regard Article XXXI. not only as containing no denial of the Mass-doctrine, but as being intended for its defence. 'Liquet igitur per hunc Articulum potius defendi quam carpi veritatem Sacrificii Eucharistici, quod Christus Dominus, tanquam perpetuam sui oblationem, Ipse per Ministros Sacerdotes usque ad sæculum consummatum in singulis oblationibus continenter facit' (p. 132).

'Doctrinam igitur catholicam de sacrificio Missæ tantum abest ut Ecclesia Anglicana repudiaverit, ut eam contra perniciosum quemdam errorem defenderit' (*ibid.*).

Another writer has more recently declared that 'Our

I am not desiring to use language which may give needless offence to any. I am sincerely sorry if I have written that which may cause unnecessary pain to anyone desiring to be a follower of Christ and to walk in the light of His truth, even though he may seem to me as yet to have some scales upon his eyes.

Let the case be stated clearly and fairly, calmly and dispassionately, without bitterness and with all loving kindness.

Fifty years ago an attempt was made to show that our Protestant Articles might be signed in a so-called 'Catholic' sense—a sense admittedly quite different from, and in some points (especially in the matter of this Article XXXI.) quite contrary to the sense they were intended to convey.

It was urged, 'We have no duties towards their framers' ('Apologia pro Vitâ Suâ,' p. 131). 'The Articles are received not in the sense of the framers, but (as far as the wording will admit or any ambiguity requires it) in the one Catholic sense' (*ibid.*).

Thirty-first Article had for its object the defence of Catholic doctrine' (*Anglican Church Magazine*, November, 1895, p. 77).

Newman felt, and—to his honour I say it—confessed (as I understand him) that, in opposing and condemning him, the authorities of the University were simply doing their duty to the traditional religion of 300 years, *i.e.*, to the religious principles of our Reformation, which they were called to defend and maintain.

Is less than this implied in the following words? 'I cannot disguise from myself that my preaching is not calculated to defend that system of religion which has been received for 300 years, and of which the heads of houses are the legitimate maintainers in this place' (*ibid.*, p. 133). 'I fear I must allow that, whether I will or no, I am disposing them (the minds of young men) towards Rome' (*ibid.*).

And now the seed which Newman was sowing then appears to be bearing fruit, which, if allowed to ripen, promises a result such as his prescience seems to have anticipated when he wrote: 'I do not think that we have yet made fair trial how much the English Church will bear. •I know it is a hazardous experiment, like proving cannon. Yet we must not take it for granted that the metal will burst in the operation. It has borne at various times, not to say at this time, a great infusion of Catholic truth without damage. As to the result, viz., whether this process will not *approximate the whole English Church, as a body, to Rome, that is nothing to us.* For what we know, it may be the providential means of *uniting the whole Church in one*, without fresh schismatizing or use of private judgment' (*ibid.*, p. 135).

And is it not then a solemn duty—would not Cardinal Newman himself have confessed that it is the duty of those who are 'the legitimate maintainers'—and something more than the legitimate maintainers—of the traditional doctrine of the Reformed Church of England, of the doctrine taught in our Articles as naturally understood and maintained by the succession of our divines—to oppose themselves to the reintroduction of those mediæval errors which our Church cast aside when conforming herself to the doctrine of Primitive Christianity, and the faith once for all delivered unto the saints?

In view of Rome's obvious additions to the faith, and the invitation to us to submit ourselves to the one supreme and infallible head of Christ's Church upon earth, is it nothing to us that we have pledged ourselves to teach nothing, as required of necessity to eternal salvation, but that which we shall be persuaded may be concluded and proved by the Scripture?

Is it nothing to us, in view of a call to put a sense on our formularies which this Church and realm confessedly hath not received, that we have solemnly bound ourselves to give faithful diligence always so to minister the doctrine and sacraments, and the discipline of Christ, as the Lord hath commanded, and as this Church and realm *hath* received the same?

Is it nothing to us, in the face of attempts to bring in again among us the sacrifices of Masses, which our Article declares to be blasphemous fables and dangerous deceits—that, at our ordination we vowed to be ready, with all faithful diligence, to banish and drive away all erroneous and strange doctrines contrary to God's word?

One thing at least is certain. The old sense —the traditional sense of 300 years—the sense in which our Reformers and our great divines upheld it—the old sense of our Thirty-first Article, can never live in peace with the new sense. To the new the old is heresy. To the old the new is blasphemy. All the less and the less will *the two views* be able to dwell together in unity (except as enfeebled by sloth, or stricken with paralysis), just in proportion as those who hold the old and those who hold the new learn more and more to love one another.

And another thing ought to be regarded as equally certain—the new wine of the novel sense can never be put in the old bottles of our English formularies without bursting them.

And yet one other thing is (as I am persuaded) not less true. No one having truly tasted the old wine—the wine of the traditional sense—the wine of the simple, ancient, apostolic faith—no one having drunk the old wine of the Gospel of Christ, and found it to be the power of God unto salvation, will straightway desire the new wine of novel doctrines, for he will say, 'The old is better.'

But, alas! it is too true that in upholding the doctrines of the Reformation we have many times been sadly content to know little of their power. Too often we have contended for the truth of the Gospel, while showing little of the glow of its light and its love!

Let us thank God that now He is moving the hearts of many to cry earnestly and mightily to Him for a quickening and reviving of the Holy Spirit's work in testifying of Christ—for showers of blessing on the testimony of missionaries abroad and faithful ministers at home, and especially for a great revival of the truth and power of the Gospel in our English universities.

He will hear, and He will answer.

He only doeth great wonders, for His mercy endureth for ever.

What a blessing to our land it will be when 'Dominus illuminatio mea' shall be graven on the heart of our universities, to be known and read of all men, and the darkness of superstition and the gloom of agnosticism shall be scattered before the light of the knowledge of the glory of God in the face of Jesus Christ!

'Now, unto Him that is able to do exceeding abundantly, above all that we ask or think, according to the power that worketh in us, unto Him be glory in the Church by Christ Jesus throughout all ages, world without end. Amen.'

NOTICE.

It has not been desired to multiply quotations without sufficient cause.

It has been judged superfluous to insert quotations—however valuable—from Puritan writers generally, seeing that their decided testimony against Romish error, and especially their strong denunciation of the Mass, is too notorious to be questioned.

If scant testimony has been given from the Reformers, it is because their writings are pretty well known to abound with it.

As regards others, one or two quotations, as a rule, have been thought to be sufficient when they have been directly to the point. But in some few cases exceptions have been made, the reason for which will probably be apparent to the reader.

I shall be thankful for the correction of any errors which may be found in the quotations, especially of any which may seem capable of conveying anything like a misapprehension.

Exception may probably be taken (and perhaps justly) to the inclusion of some of the later writers quoted among divines of the Church of England. But it was thought very desirable to show by some prominent examples that after the nonjurors had felt themselves compelled to secede from the Church of their fathers, and take their eccentric (and, in some cases, extravagant) views into a separate communion of their own, they still taught a doctrine of the Eucharistic sacrifice which was clearly and widely separate from the Tridentine teaching, and as distinctly and strongly as ever opposed to the Romish Mass (see Lathbury's 'History of the Nonjurors,' pp. 94-103, 360).

TESTIMONIES OF ENGLISH DIVINES.

Tyndale.

'And when he saith, "The priest offereth, or sacrificeth, Christ's body," I answer, "Christ was offered once for all," as it is to see in the Epistle to the Hebrews. . . .

'Let no man beguile you with his juggling sophistry. Our offering of Christ is to believe in Him, and to come with a repenting heart unto the remembrance of His passion; and to desire God the Father for the breaking of Christ's body on the Cross, and shedding of His blood, and for His death, and all His passions, to be merciful unto us, and to forgive us, according to His testament and promise; and so we receive forgiveness of our sins. And other offering or sacrificing of Christ is there none. Walk in the open light and feeling; and let not yourselves be led with juggling words, as mules and asses, in which there is none understanding' (Answer to Sir Thomas More, ch. x., p. 149. P.S. edit.).

Bishop Geste.

I.

'Paul saith not with a manifold or renewed but with one offering hath Christ made perfect for ever the sanctified, in consideration whereof they be foul deceived who avouch Christ's sacrifice ought to be revived and multiplied to the full pardon and contentation of our sin otherwise unpardonable, and therefore repeat the said sacrifice day by day to the same effect, for why that, that is oft offered cannot justly be recounted to be offered but once, by reason a repeated and renewed sacrifice is not merely single and one, but manifold and diverse' ('Against the Privy Mass,' pp. 77, 78. 1548. In Dugdale's 'Life of Geste,' p. 88).

II.

'The next entretable matter is that the said sacrifice is nothing available either for the quick or the dead. Our Catholics contend it is profitable for them both' (*ibid.*, p. 96).

III.

'To attempt to offer Christ as it is an enterprise too bold and presumptuous, so unsufferable and *blasphemous*' (*ibid.*, p. 100).

IV.

'I have argued (I suppose forcibly) the priest-sacrifice to be neither propitiatory nor available, neither godly nor approvable, but *sinful and unsufferable*' (*ibid.*, p. 103).

V.

'The true Mass, otherwise named the Communion, which cannot be so highly esteemed and so often frequented, as of necessity it ought, without the priest-mass be *hated* and *detested*, for both *it and the communion cannot be jointly regarded*. Whoso loveth the one must needs hate the other, for why, they be *mere contraries*' (*ibid.*, pp. 139, 140).

CRANMER.

1.

'The offering of the priest in the Mass, or the appointing of his ministration at his pleasure, to them that be quick or dead, cannot merit or deserve, neither to himself nor to them for whom he singeth or saith, the remission of their sins ... such popish doctrine is contrary to the doctrine of the Gospel, and injurious to the sacrifice of Christ. For if only the death of Christ be the oblation, sacrifice, and price wherefore our sins be pardoned, then the act or ministration of the priest cannot have the same office. Wherefore it is an abominable *blasphemy* to give that office or dignity to a priest, which pertaineth only to Christ' (on the 'Lord's Supper,' P.S., p. 348).

II.

'The rest is but branches and leaves, the cutting away whereof is but like topping and lopping of a tree, or cutting down of weeds, leaving the body standing, and the roots in the ground; but the very body of the tree, or rather the roots of the weeds, is the popish doctrine of transubstantiation, and of the real presence of Christ's flesh and blood in the sacrament of the altar (as they call it), and of the sacrifice and oblation of Christ, made by the priest for the salvation of the quick and the dead, which roots, if they be suffered to grow in the Lord's vineyard, they will overspread all the ground again with the old errors and superstitions' (Preface to 'Lord's Supper,' 1550).

RIDLEY.

I.

'They pluck away the honour from the only sacrifice of Christ, whilst the sacramental and Mass sacrifice is believed to be propitiatory, and such a one as purgeth the souls, both of the quick and the dead' (Works, P.S., p. 107).

II.

'Is set up a new and *blasphemous* kind of sacrifice . . . to the great and intolerable contumely of Christ our Saviour, His death, and passion' (*ibid.*, p. 52).

HUTCHINSON.

'Christ's everlasting priesthood hath made an end of all the Levites' priesthood; yea, and of all other priesthood, save only that which belongeth to all Christian men. The oblation of

His body once for all upon the altar of the Cross, which was a slain sacrifice for our sins, abolisheth all other. . . . That the Lord's supper, which men call the Mass, is not a sacrifice for sin, St. Paul declareth plainly, saying, "*Sine sanguinis effusione,*" etc. . . . The parable of the thieves teacheth us that Christ's coming hath disannulled all such priesthood as is called *sacerdotium*; but *presbyterium* remaineth' (Works, P.S., pp. 46, 48, 49).

Bishop Hooper.

I.

'Exemplum vero neotericorum impietatis aliud non quæram quam hoc, quo dicunt Christum quotidie in illorum missis ac illorum opera pro peccatis vivorum et mortuorum offerri. Joannes dicet quod Christus emundat nos ab omni peccato. Ergo totum redemptionis omnium peccatorum nostrorum pretium sanguini Christi super crucem effuso assignat; et sacrificulis nullam partem relinquit. . . . Si neoteri easdem offerunt in missis hostias, nempe corpus, sanguinem et animam quæ Christus in cruce obtulit, Christi hostiam immolationem infirmitatis arguunt: quod est omnino satanicum et impium' (Later Writings, P.S., p. 513).

II.

'Cœna Domine (quod *impia missa* non est) etiam sacrificium Christianorum vocatur, non re ipsâ, sed nominis communicatione et participatione; quia recordatio et memoria sit veri sacrificii Christi semel in cruce oblati' (Later Writings, P.S. edit., p. 394).

HADDON.

'Ubi Christus in cœna unquam sacrificium instituit sui corporis? . . . Ubi tensis ad cœlum brachiis, hostiam ad placandum Patrem obtulit? . . . Quid Apostoli? . . . Ubi pro vivis ac defunctis litabant? . . . Breviter tota hæc actionis vestræ institutio quantum a primis Apostolorum vestigiis dissiliat, quam nihil commune cum communione Christi, nihil cum sacra illius cœna conjunctum præ se ferat, vel orbis Christianorum judicet . . . Sacramentum primum vertistis in sacrificium, mensam in aram commutastis, Mysteria in Missas, cœnationem in adorationem transtulistis, communionem in cultum, epulum in spectaculum. . . . Denique eò rem produxistis, ut ne cœnæ quidem ulla vel species, aut nomen in templis permaneat' (' Contra Osorium,' lib. iii., fol. 358a, London, 1577).

JEWEL.

'They did tell us that in their Mass they were able to make Christ the Son of God, and to offer Him unto God His Father for our sins. O *blasphemous speech*, and *most injurious* to the glorious work of our redemption. . . . Such kind of sacrifice we have not. . . . It is the blood of Jesus Christ which cleanseth us from all sin. This is our sacrifice, this is our propitiation, this is the propitiation and sacrifice for the whole world. How, then, saith Pope Pius we have no sacrifice?' ('View of Seditious Bull,' Works, P.S. Defence, etc., pp. 1139, 1140).

COVERDALE.

'Let us look, wherefore they call it a sacrifice. Even because, say they, that in the Mass Christ the Son is offered up unto God His Father.

Oh, what a *great blasphemy* is this; yea, to be abhorred of all virtuous men!' ('Remains,' P.S. edit., p. 470).

The Archbishops, Bishops, and Ministers of 1560.

'Missa, ut consuevit a Sacerdotibus dici, non erat a Christo instituta, sed a multis Romanis Pontificibus consarcinata. Nec est sacrificium propitiatorium pro vivis et defunctis' ('Articles of the Principal Heads of Religion').*

The Archbishops and Bishops of 1560.

'The doctrine that maintaineth the Mass to be a propitiatory sacrifice for the quick and the dead, and a means to deliver souls out of purgatory, is neither agreeable to Christ's ordinance, nor grounded upon doctrine apostolic. But contrariwise, most ungodly and most injurious to the

---

* To these Articles the ministers were to subscribe in the following form: 'Hæc omnia vera esse et publice docenda profitemur . . . . Hancque nostram confessionem manuum nostrarum subscriptionibus testificamur, contrariamque doctrinam abolendam esse judicamus, et detestamur' (see Strype's 'Annals,' vol. i., ch. xvii., p. 217).

precious redemption of our Saviour Christ, and His only-sufficient sacrifice offered once for ever upon the altar of the Cross' ('Declaration . . . for the Unity of Doctrine,' to be read publicly by all ministers upon their first coming into their benefices).*

Bishop T. Cooper (of Winchester).

I.

'I will . . show you out of your own authors, what I take your private Mass to be. It is a sacrifice of the body and blood of Christ, used in the Church in the place of the Lord's Supper, by one priest alone offered to God the Father for the sins of quick and dead' ('Defence of the Truth,' pp. 57, 58, P.S. edit.).

II.

'The priest (say you) is bound to offer up the daily sacrifice for himself and for the people. This is the root of all the abuses of the Lord's

---

* See Strype's 'Annals,' vol. i., ch. xvii., p. 219. London, 1725. This declaration went forth in the general name of both Metropolitans and all the bishops; but (according to Strype, Parker's 'Life,' p. 92) seems to have been chiefly the work of Parker.

Supper that ye have brought into the Church of Christ' (*ibid.*, p. 87).

III.

'The Lord's Supper is a remembrance of one perfect sacrifice, whereby we were once sufficiently purged from sin, and continually are revived by the same; your sacrifice is a daily offering up of Christ for our sins, as though it had not been perfectly done at the first' (*ibid.*, p. 98).

IV.

'So much difference is there between the sacrament by Christ appointed, and the sacrifice of the Mass by you devised' (*ibid.*, p. 99).

The Archbishops and Bishops in the Realm of Ireland and others in 1566.

'The doctrine which maintaineth the Mass to be a propitiatory sacrifice for the quick and the dead, and a mean to deliver souls from purgatory, is neither agreeable to Christ's ordinance, nor grounded upon doctrine Apostolic, but contrariwise most ungodly and most injurious to the precious redemption of our Saviour Christ and His only sufficient sacrifice offered once for ever upon the altar of the Cross' (see Ussher's Works, Elrington's edit., vol. i., p. xxviii.).

Archbishop Parker and other Bishops between 1566 and 1570.*

'In this sermon here published some things be spoken *not consonant to sound doctrine*, but rather to such corruption of great *ignorance and superstition*, as hath taken root in the Church of long time, being overmuch combered with monckery. As when it speaketh of *the Mass to be profitable to the quick and dead*' († Preface to 'Homily of Ælfric,' signed not only by Parker, but by the Archbishop of York, the Bishop of London, and twelve other bishops).

Bishop Pilkington.

'For their sacrifice of the Mass, that he so much laments to be defaced, and all good consciences rejoice that God of His undeserved

---

* See Introduction in Thomson's edit. (pp. iii., iv.) of the 'Testimony of Antiquity.'

† See Appendix, note A.

goodness has overthrown it, I refer all men to the fifth and last book that the blessed souls now living with God, Bishops Cranmer and Ridley, wrote of the sacrament, whose bodies they cruelly tormented therefor' (Works, P.S. edit., pp. 547, 548).

Dean Nowell.

'M. *An fuit instituta a Christo cœna, ut Deo Patri hostia pro peccatis expiandis immolaretur?*

'A. Minime : nam Christus mortem in cruce occumbens, unicum illud sempiternum sacrificium semel in perpetuum pro nostra salute obtulit' (Christianæ pietatis prima institutio, ad usum Scholarum Græce et Latine Scripta.* London, 1577. 'Cum Gratia et Privilegio,' fol. 101 *b*).

* This is Nowell's 'Middle Catechism,' concerning which see Churton's 'Life of Nowell,' pp. 188, *sqq*. It had a very extensive circulation in the reign of Elizabeth, and continued to be used in schools for a century or more. In the reign of Queen Anne an English edition was published, for which Mr. Nelson had readily consented to write a commendatory preface. But his lamented death prevented him from fulfilling his design. See Churton's 'Life,' pp. 193, 194. The teaching of the smaller Catechism is equally strong. See *ibid.*, p. 419.

Archbishop Grindal.

I.

'Christ gave a sacrament to strengthen men's faith; the priest giveth a sacrifice to redeem men's souls. Christ gave it to be eaten; the priest giveth it to be worshipped. . . . Thus you may see that the Massing-priest receiveth the sacrament of Christ's body far otherwise than ever Christ minded; and so, therefore, unworthily and to his condemnation' ('Remains,' P.S. edit., pp. 57, 58).

II.

'The Mass is forbidden in the Scripture, as thus: It was thought to be meritorious, it did take away free justification, it was made an idol, and idolatry is forbidden in the Scriptures' (*ibid.*, pp. 211, 212).

Archbishop Sandys.

I.

'In the Scriptures, wherein is contained all that is good, and all that which God requireth or accepteth of, we find no mention either of the name or of the thing of the Mass ... either any such popish trash' ('Sermons,' P.S. edit., p. 223).

II.

'Where the popish priesthood taketh footing, in what ground the foundation thereof is laid, I cannot find in the Scriptures. Anti-Christ is the author of that priesthood. ... The priest, according to the order of Melchizedeck, hath offered the sacrifice of His own flesh, acceptable even for the worthiness of it, and by the virtue which is in it forcible and more than sufficient to wash away all sin. ... He did it perfectly. ... Where full remission of sin is, there needeth no further sacrifice for sin; and the Holy Ghost beareth us record that we have full remission of all our sins. ... "The blood of Jesus cleanseth us from all sin"; the blood of Jesus *once* shed, the offering of the body of Jesus Christ *once*. So that there remaineth no other sacrifice to be daily offered, but the sacrifice of "righteousness," which we must all offer' (*ibid.*, pp. 411, 412).

Fulke.

I.

'The word *priest*, by popish abuse, is commonly taken for a sacrificer. . . . But the Holy Ghost never calleth the ministers of the word and sacraments of the New Testament ἱερεῖς or *sacerdotes*. . . . The name of priest, according to the original derivation from *presbyter*, we do not refuse; but according to the common acception for a *sacrificer* we cannot take it, when it is spoken of the ministry of the New Testament'* ('Defence of Translation,' P.S. edit., p. 119).

II.

'In denying the *blasphemous* sacrifice of the popish Mass, with the altar and priesthood that thereto belongeth, we use no wily policy, but with open mouth at all times, and in all places, we cry *out upon it*' (*ibid.*, p. 241).

---

* This distinction will be found constantly recurring in the writings of English divines. Bishop King (in the reign of James I.), of London, acknowledging that we 'allow no other priesthood nor other priest but Christ' (in his dealing with John Almond), and answering 'No,' to the Benedictine Scott's question, 'Are *you* a priest?' explained himself thus: 'I am a priest, but not a Massing-priest' (see Hutton's 'Anglican Ministry,' pp. 515, 516).

Whitaker.

'Hoc sacrificium . . . semel oblatum Deo Patri pro peccatis nostris cumulatissime satisfecit : ergo non opus est ut repetatur, et qui repeti volunt Christo summam contumeliam faciunt, quasi non præstiterit, quod in se susceperit. At Papistica Ecclesia hoc sacrificium sæpe rependendum esse statuit. Sic Concilium Tridentinum, sess. 22, cap. i. Quare manifestum est, Papistas Christum Ejusque sacrificium longe augustissimum *horrendâ contumeliâ* afficere' ('Prælectiones,' pp. 475, 476. Cambridge, 1599).

Bishop Alley.

I.

'We cannot well grant that they, in their masking Mass, offer any such sacrifice, for they boast that they offer *reale corpus, et realem sanguinem*, as they term it. The holy Father Irenæus doth write, that the thing that is offered receiveth his dignity and worthiness of him that doth offer, and that the sacrifice is accepted of God, because he that offereth it is accepted of God. Upon this I make argument: Every person that doth offer is of more worthiness than the thing which he offereth. The priest doth offer the body of Christ: *ergo*, the priest is of more worthiness than the body of Christ. O blasphemy intolerable!' (Πτωχομουσείον. 'The Poor Man's Library,' tom. i., fol. 218 *a*. Edit. Day, 1565).

II.

'We shall not find in the Holy Scriptures that the ministers of the New Testament be called either *Sacerdotes* or *Sacrifici*. For that is attributed wholly and only unto Christ' (*ibid.*, tom. ii., fol. 36 *b*).

Archbishop Whitgift.

I.

'St. Augustine . . . speaketh against such as, professing Christianity, did, notwithstanding, resort to the temples of the Pagans at their solemnities and feasts . . . much like unto those that think it sufficient to serve God in heart, though in body they be present *at the Mass and idolatrous service*. . . . It was in St. Augustine's time, as it is in some places at this day, where in some one city there be churches both for the Gospel, and for the Mass also : it is not meet that such as profess the Gospel should *resort to the Mass;* for besides that they offend God in being present at *idolatrous service*, they also give occasion to the papists to think better of their Mass' ('Defence of Answer to Admonition,' Tract vii., ch. v., div. 3. Works, P.S., vol. ii., p. 34).

II.

'As for the name of priest, as they took it [*i.e.*, as sacrificers], he did likewise condemn in our ministers, neither did they ascribe it to themselves. And that, therefore, the libeller in these points writ like himself' (Strype, 'Life of Whitgift,' p. 305. London, 1718).

III.

'The very word [priest] itself, as it is used in our English tongue, soundeth the word *presbyter*. As heretofore use hath made it to be taken for a *sacrificer*, so will use now alter that signification, and make it to be taken for a minister of the Gospel' (Works, P.S., vol. iii., p. 351. See 'Eucharistic Presence,' pp. 30, 31).

HOOKER.

I.

'He which saith, "Depart out of Babylon, lest ye be partakers of her sins," sheweth plainly that He meaneth such sins, as except we separate ourselves, we have no power in the world to avoid such *impieties* as by law they have established. . . . As for example, in the Church of Rome it is maintained . . . that the bread in the Eucharist is transubstantiated into Christ; that it is to be adored, and *to be offered up unto God as a sacrifice propitiatory for quick and dead*' ('Discourse of Justification,' § 11, Works, vol. iii., pp. 497, 498. Edit. Keble).

II.

'Tell not us . . . that ye will read our Scriptures, if we will listen to your traditions; that if ye may have a Mass by permission, we shall have a Communion with good leave and liking. . . . Solomon took it (as well he might) for an evident proof that she did not bear a motherly affection to her child which yielded to have it cut in divers parts. He cannot love the Lord Jesus with his heart, which lendeth one ear to His apostles and another to false apostles; which can brook to see a mingle-mangle of religion and superstition, *ministers and massing-priests*, light and darkness, truth and error, traditions and Scriptures. No, we have no lord but Jesus, no doctrine but the Gospel, no teachers but His apostles' ('Sermon on St. Jude's Epistle,' Works, vol. iii., p. 666. Edit. Keble).

III.

'Touching the ministry of the Gospel of Jesus Christ; the whole body of the Church being divided into laity and clergy, the clergy are either presbyters or deacons. I rather term the one sort *presbyters* than *priests*, because in a matter of so small moment I would not willingly offend their ears to whom the name of priesthood is odious, though without cause. . . . Howbeit, because the most eminent part both of heathenish and Jewish service did consist in sacrifice, when learned men declare that the word *priest* doth properly signify according to the mind of the first imposer of that name, their ordinary scholics do well expound it to imply *sacrifice*. *Seeing** *then that sacrifice is now no part of the Church*

---

* On this statement see 'Eucharistic Presence,' pp. 31, 32.

ministry, how should the name of priesthood be thereunto rightly applied? Surely, even as St. Paul applieth the name of flesh unto that very substance of fishes which hath a proportionable correspondence to flesh, although it be in nature another thing . . . the word presbyter doth seem more fit, and in propriety of speech more agreeable than priest with the drift of the whole Gospel of Jesus Christ. . . . The Holy Ghost throughout the body of the New Testament making no such mention of them doth not anywhere call them priests. The prophet Esay I grant doth, but in such sort as the ancient fathers, by way of analogy' ('Eccl. Pol.,' Book V., ch. lxxviii., § 2, 3. Works, vol. ii., pp. 469-472. Edit. Keble).

Archbishop Bancroft.

I.

'Out of these books [of pretended Reformers], because some might otherwise charge the premises herein with slander of the godly brethren, I have thought it very convenient to lay down before you, particularly, some most lewd and wicked speeches.

'Some of their consistorial sayings, as touching our religion, Communion-book, sacraments and ceremonies. . . . *They eat not the Lord's Supper, but play a pageant of their own, to blind the people, and keep them still in superstition: to make the silly souls believe that they have an English Mass: and so put no difference betwixt truth and falsehood, betwixt Christ and Antichrist*' ('Dangerous Positions,' pp. 46, 47, 50, 56. London, 1593).

'Their especial drift in their said railing speeches, as outrageously published, as if they were mere Jesuits, and peradventure to as dangerous a purpose' (*ibid.*, p. 61).

II.

'They [the Papists] forbid the reading of the Scriptures; and the better to be obeyed, they will not permit the Scriptures in the vulgar tongue. . . . [The people therefore are drawn] from the sure trust and confidence in His Death to Masses, pardons, and I know not what intolerable superstition and idolatry' ('Sermon,' 1588, p. 36. See Lathbury's 'Hist. of Convocation,' p. 254).

Dean Field.

I.

'The very form and words of the Liturgy condemn the abuse of private masses and half-communion, and make nothing of that propitiatory sacrifice whereof the papists fable, which are those greatest mysteries of Romish religion that they insist upon in their Mass' ('Of the Church,' Book III., Appendix, vol. ii., p. 22, E.H.S.)

II.

'The best and principal men that then (*i.e.*, before Luther) lived, taught peremptorily that Christ is not newly offered any otherwise than in that He is offered to the view* of God, nor any

---

* Field's language concerning 'offering' has led to so much misunderstanding (see, *e.g.*, Canon T. T. Carter in 'Correspondence with Marriott,' p. 92) that it seems desirable to quote the following passage, which may serve as an explanation not only of his own words, but of similar language used by other writers: 'Touching the manner of offering Christ's body and blood, we must consider that there is a double offering of a thing to God. First, so as men are wont to do that give something to God out of that they possess, professing that they will no longer be owners of it, but that it shall be His, and serve for such uses and employments as He shall convert it to. Secondly, a man may be said to offer a thing to God in that he bringeth it to His presence, setteth it before His eyes and *offereth it to His*

otherwise sacrificed than in that His sacrifice on the Cross is commemorated and represented' ('Of the Church,' Book III., Appendix, vol. ii., p. 72, E.H.S.).

III.

'Wherefore, from this point of Romish religion . . . let us come to the next, which is the propitiatory sacrifice for the quick and the dead. . . . I will make it appear that the Canon of the Mass importeth no such sacrifice, and . . . I will show at large, that neither before nor after Luther's *view*, to incline Him to do something by the sight of it and respect had to it. In this sort Christ offereth Himself and His body once crucified daily in heaven, and so intercedeth for us; not as giving it in the nature of a gift or present, for He gave Himself to God *once*, to be holy unto Him for ever; *nor in the nature of a sacrifice*, for He died *once* for sin, and rose again never to die any more; but in that He setteth it before the eyes of God His Father, representing it unto Him, and *so offering it to His view* to obtain grace and mercy for us. And *in this sort* we also offer Him daily on the altar, in that, commemorating His death and lively representing His bitter passion endured in His body upon the Cross, *we offer* Him that was once crucified and sacrificed for us on the Cross, and all His sufferings, *to the view and gracious consideration of the Almighty*, earnestly desiring and assuredly hoping that He will incline to pity us and show mercy unto us, for this His dearest Son's sake, who in our nature, for us, to satisfy His displeasure and to procure us acceptation, endured such and so grievous things' ('Of the Church,' Book III., Appendix, vol. ii., p. 62, E.H.S.). See below, Appendix, note B.

appearing, the Church believed, nor knew any such new real sacrificing of Christ, as is now imagined' ('Of the Church,' Book III., Appendix, vol. ii., p. 59, E.H.S.).

IV.

'I say briefly . . . that we have altars in some sort as the Fathers had, though we have thrown down popish altars; that we admit the Eucharist to be rightly named a sacrifice, though we detest the *blasphemous* construction the papists make of it' (*ibid.*, p. 83).

V.

'It is made clear and evident, that the best and worthiest amongst the guides of God's Church before Luther's time taught, as we do, that the sacrifice of the altar is only the sacrifice of praise and thanksgiving, and a mere representation and commemoration of the sacrifice once offered on the Cross; and consequently are all put under the curse, and anathematized by the Tridentine Council' ('Of the Church,' Book III., Appendix, vol. ii., p. 94, E.H.S.).

ROGERS.

'We are to note, first, *blasphemous fables.* For it is a fable that the Mass is a sacrifice, and that propitiatory . . . a fable that one and the same sacrifice is offered in the Mass which was offered on the Cross; a fable, that the said Mass is any whit profitable for the quick, much less for the dead. Next, *dangerous deceits.* For hereby men are taught to believe that creatures may be adored; contrary to God's Word. Christ is often offered; contrary to the Scripture. The priest offereth up Christ; contrary to the Scripture. . . . All which their fables and deceits do tend to the utter abolishing of true religion. Therefore justly have we and our godly brethren abandoned the Mass' ('The Faith, Doctrine and Religion professed and protected in the Realm of England. . . . Perused, and by the lawful authority of the Church of England allowed to be public. 1607.' P.S. edit., pp. 300, 301).

WILLET.

I.

'We deny not, but that the sacrament may be called a sacrifice, that is, a spiritual oblation of praise and thanksgiving; but that there is a proper and external sacrifice, as in the law of goats and bullocks, upon the Cross of the Body of Christ; so in the Eucharist, of the same Body and Flesh of Christ, we do hold it for a great *blasphemy* and heresy' (Willet's 'Synopsis Papismi,' vol. v., p. 352. London, 1852).

II.

'We hold it to be a great *blasphemy* to say that the priesthood and sacrifice of Christ upon the Cross is not that sacrifice or priesthood into the which the old sacrifice and priesthood was translated and changed' (*ibid.*, p. 364).

III.

'Concerning the name of priests in their sense, as it implieth an authority of sacrificing, we utterly *abhor*. . . . To conclude, this word *priest*, as it is the English of *sacerdos*, we do not approve; but as it giveth the sense of *presbyter*, from whence it is derived, we condemn it not' (*ibid.*, p. 365).

IV.

'They *blasphemously* affirm that it is a sacrifice propitiatory' (*ibid.*, p. 368).

Bishop Bilson.

I.

'You will have a real, corporal, and local proffering of Christ's flesh to God the Father under the forms of bread and wine made by the priest's external actions and gestures for the sins of such as he list: this is, we say, a *wicked* and *blasphemous* mockery. His passion is the true oblation of the Church; His flesh wounded and blood shed are the only sacrifices for sin' ('True Difference,' p. 700. Oxford, 1585).

II.

'*Philander* [Jesuit].—As though the ancient Fathers did not also say that Christ is daily offered in the Church.

'*Theophilus* [Christian].—Not in the *substance*, which is your error, but in *signification*, which is their doctrine and ours. Take their interpretation with their words, and they make nothing for your local and external offering of Christ. . . . The Catholic Fathers I can assure you say, *Christ is offered* and *Christ is crucified* in the Lord's supper indifferently' (*ibid.*, pp. 690, 691).

Bishop Robert Abbott.

I.

'*Singulari et solo vero sacrificio Christi pro nobis sanguis effusus est, sanguis innocens, quo nocentium omnia peccata delevit* (Aug.). Quare *unum verum sacerdotem agnoscimus, mediatorem Dei et hominum, qui altare Dei vero sacrificio solus implevit* (Aug.), *nec præter ipsum alteri cuipiam homini sive sacerdotii nomen, sive rem ipsam ascribimus* (Cyril. Ep. 10 ad Nestor.). Tale enim est Christi sacerdotium, ut *ad alium transire non possit*. . . . Blasphemia est ergo quod sacrificium Missæ nuncupatur, et cœna Domini non proprie sacrificium, sed *magis recordatio sacrificii* interpretanda est, nec vere ibi Christus offertur, *magis autem oblationis illius memoriam facimus, perinde ac esset* (reipsa ergo non est) *hoc tempore immolatus* (Theophylact. in Heb. x.). *Passio est enim Christi sacrificium quod offerimus* (Cyprian). Qualis ergo ibi passio, tale sacrificium : passio tantummodo figurata est ; non aliud ergo sacrificium. *Verum namque et reale sacrificium veram et realem mortem aut destructionem rei immolatæ desiderat* (Bellarm. De Missa, Lib. I., c. 27). Quia ergo in Eucharistia vera et realis mors vel destructio Christi esse non potest (quo nodo solvendo Bellarminus se plane ridendum dat) idcirco in Eucharistia verum et reale Christi sacrificium affirmari non debet. *Supplicationes* ergo *et gratiarum actiones solæ nunc Deo charæ victimæ, et has solas Christiani facere didicerunt, etiam in illa quæ alimento sicco et humido* (panis et vini) *perficitur commemoratione, in qua passionis Filii Dei memoria servatur* (Justin Mart.)' ('Antilogia adv. Apologiam pro Garneto,' p. 70. London, 1613).

II.

'For that propitiatory sacrifice which he driveth at is beyond God's device; God never taught it, Christ never ordained it, the Primitive Church never intended it; there is no reason at all for it, because the blood of Christ once shed for us is a sufficient propitiation and atonement for all our sins. And because by *once offering of Himself He hath purged our sins, and made us perfect for ever*, therefore it is no despite to God's true worship, but a just assertion thereof, to hold that the pretence of any further sacrifice for sin is an *impious* and *blasphemous* derogation to the Cross of Christ' ('Defence of Reformed Catholic,' part iii., p. 171. London, 1609).

III.

'The *passion* of Christ is the sacrifice which we offer; and because the *passion* of Christ is not now really acted, therefore the sacrifice which we offer is no *true* and *real* sacrifice' ('Counterproof against Dr. Bishop,' c. xiv., p. 364. See Waterland's Works, vol. v., p. 141).

BISHOP BABINGTON.

I.

'*It is finished*, and why are we feared? . . . See, see *their sin* that devise a daily sacrifice for sin, either adding unto this most perfect redemption as if it wanted, or else vainly doing by a work of will what already is fully done by prescript of God. . . . The virtue, power, and efficacy of this sacrifice is perpetual, being once made, and needeth but by faith to be taken hold of and applied' ('Exposition of Lord's Prayer,' Petition I., p. 26. London, 1615).

II.

'The Mass casteth upon our Saviour this reproach, that He is not the only Priest of the

New Testament. . . . It overthroweth the merit of His death and passion. . . . The errors and *blasphemies* that are to be found in the Canon of the Mass show how truly detestable it is and ought to be to all faithful men and women ever' ('Exposition of Catholic Faith,' pp. 255, 256. London, 1615).

Archdeacon Mason.

I.

'Vos aliud cerebri vestri figmentum adjecitis, potestatem scilicet offerendi sacrificium proprie dictum, et proprie *propitiatorium* pro vivis et defunctis. In qua fieri non potest, ut vos Apostolis succedatis, cum nec ipsi (ut postea liquebit) tales fuerint sacerdotes, nec ullum unquam istiusmodi sacerdotium posteris tradiderint' ('Vindiciæ Ecclesiæ Anglicanæ,'* Lib. II., c. i., p. 59. London, 1625).

II.

'Docet Concilium Tridentinum in Missa, *offerri Deo verum et proprium Sacrificium*. . . . Eccle-

---

* On Bishop Overall's connection with this work, see 'Papers on Eucharistic Presence,' p. 303.

sia Anglicana longe rectius docet. . . . Missas pro vivis et defunctis *blasphemas esse fabulas, et periculosas imposturas.* Hujusmodi igitur sacrificium missaticum, ad Ministros Evangelicos spectare non agnoscimus' (*ibid.*, Lib. V., c. i., p. 545).

III.

'Nos . . . Sacerdotium vestrum missificum, non modo humanum esse commentum, sed etiam in conspectu ipsius Dei viventis *sacrilegum*, et *abominandum* probavimus' (*ibid.*, p. 660).

Bishop William Cowper (of Galloway).

'I pray you mark how *blasphemous and deceitful* a thing their Mass is. First, is not this a mockery of God the Father, to desire Him to accept His own Son? Is Christ out of the favour of His Father? Said He not, He is My Son, in whom I am well pleased? Shall a mortal and miserable sinful priest be a mediator or peacemaker between the Father and the Son, praying the Father that He would accept His Son, and send down an angel to take up His body into heaven?

'R. Fie upon it. It is a *vile blasphemy*.

'C. Secondly, see you not how it inverts God's ordinance? for where He hath ordained a sacrament, wherein God offers and gives His Son to us, they have changed it into a *sacrifice*, wherein they offer up the Son to the Father.

'R. I see that also.

'C. Thirdly, is it not an *injurious* thing to Christ to say that any can offer Him up to God but Himself?

'R. It is indeed; for as no other sacrifice can satisfy God's justice, so no other sacrificer can be worthy to offer Him but Himself, as is clear out of your former testimonies.

'C. Fourthly, is it not a deceiving of the people to say, that an unbloody sacrifice (such as they say the Mass is) can be propitiatory to obtain remission of sins?

'R. It is, indeed; and expressly against the Word of God you have alleged, *Without shedding of blood there is no remission.* They grant themselves, that in the Mass there is no shedding of blood, and how then can it give pardon or remission of sins?' ('Seven Days' Conference, Day 6,' Works, pp. 673, 674. London, 1629.)

King James I.

I.

'Veteris Ecclesiæ Patres sacrificium in religione Christiana unum agnovisse, quod in locum successit omnium legis Mosaicæ sacrificiorum, neque ignorat Rex, neque negat. Sed hoc sacrificium nihil esse aliud contendit, nisi commemorationem ejus, quod semel in cruce Christus Patri suo obtulit' ('Responsio ad Epist. Card. Perronii, ab Isaaco Casaubano, sereniss. Rege dictante, scripta,' obs. v. In 'Jacobi Regis Angliæ Op. Reg.,' p. 188. Francofurti ad Moenum, 1689).

II.

'Eucharistiæ celebrationem sine communicantibus, et universam illam privatarum missarum nundinationem, multis etiam vestrorum theologis damnatam, certum est a perversa doctrina de hoc sacrificio originem habuisse. Quod autem ad extrahendas Defunctorum animas e flammis Purgatorii sacrificia missarum exiguntur, et quidem sæpe repetita; otiosorum hominum et simplicitate populorum ad quæstum suum impie abutentium, dilirium esse, Rex non dubitat. Tollantur hi et similes his alii crassi fœdique abusus, qui apud vos obtinent'* (*ibid.*, pp. 188, 189).

Bishop Andrewes.

'Hoc est quod *mirantur* nostri homines: non quod mirari ibi eos fingit Cardinalis. Credunt enim, institutam a Domino Eucharistiam in sui commemorationem; etiam sacrificii sui, vel (si ita loqui liceat) *in sacrificium commemorativum;* non autem in sacramentum modo, vel alimoniam spiritualem. Hoc quidem etsi admittant, negant tamen utrumque usum hunc (sic a Domino simul et conjunctim institutum) divelli posse ab homine, aut propter vel populi negligentiam, vel sacerdotum avaritiam, alterum ab altero abrumpi. *Sacrificium*, quod ibi est, *Eucharisticum* esse: cujus sacrificii ea lex, ut qui illud offerat, de eo participet: participet autem accipiendo et comedendo (uti jusset Servator). Nam *participare impetrando, nuperum* id quidem et *novitium* participandi genus; ac multo enim magis quam Missa illa privata. . . . At vos tollite de Missâ Transubstantiationem vestram; nec diu nobiscum

---

* Compare below, p. 116, see Pattison's ' Isaac Casaubon,' pp. 322, 347, 348; and compare Casaubon's ' Exercitationes,' pp. 575, 576, 580. London, 1614.

lis erit de sacrificio. *Memoriam* ibi fieri *sacrificii,* damus non inviti. *Sacrificari ibi Christum restrum de pane factum,* nunquam daturi. *Sacrificii* vocem scit [Rex] Patribus usurpatam, nec ponit inter res novas : at *restri in Missâ sacrificii,* et audet, et ponit' ('Ad Bellarm. Responsio,' pp. 250, 251, A.C.L., p. 184 of previous edition).

Bishop Buckeridge.

I.

'De sacrificio item *commemorativo,* sive *representativo,* quo Christus ipse qui in cruce pro nobis immolatus est, per viam representationis et commemorationis a nobis etiam *quodammodo offerri* dicitur, lis non magna est ; in Baptismo enim offertur sacrificium Christi, uti Augustinus,' etc. ('De Potest. Papæ in præf.,' quoted from Waterland, Works, vol. v., p. 137. Oxford, 1843).

II.

'The only sacrifice, one in itself, and *once only offered.* . . . And the true sacrifice . . . this only hath power to appease God's wrath. . . And the proper sacrifice . . . He took flesh of ours that He might offer for us. . . . He cannot be offered again no more than He can be dead again

... and therefore, though in the Cross and the Eucharist there be *idem sacrificatum*, "the same sacrificed thing," that is, the body and blood of Christ offered by Christ to His Father on the Cross, and received and participated by the communicants in the sacrifice of the altar, yet *idem sacrificium quoad actionem sacrificii*, or *sacrificandi*, it is impossible there should be the same sacrifice, understanding by sacrifice the action of the sacrifice. For then the action of Christ's sacrifice, which is *long since past*, should continue as long as the Eucharist shall endure, even unto the world's end, and His *consummatum est* is not yet finished; and dying and not dying, shedding of blood and not shedding of blood, and suffering and not suffering, *cannot possibly be one action;* and the *representation* of an action cannot be the *action itself*" (see Andrewes's Works, vol. v., p. 260, A.C.L.).

III.

'When he saith it is a representative or commemorative sacrifice, *respectu præteriti*, "in respect of that which is past," that is, the passion of Christ which was the true sacrifice, he doth deny by consequent that it is the true sacrifice itself which is past. And if Christ be sacrificed daily in the Eucharist, according to the action of sacrifice, and it be one and the same sacrifice offered by Christ on the Cross and the priest at the altar, then can it not be a representation of that sacrifice which is past, because it is one and the same sacrifice and action present' (*ibid.*, p. 262).

CRAKANTHORP.

I.

'Ex his quæ jam de Transubstantiatione vestrâ declaravimus, præter multa alia duo consequuntur. Prius est, *Sacrificium Missæ non esse sacrificium propitiatorium*, ut Concilium Tridentinum definit, vestrique docent. . . . Sacrificium tale nullum vel unquam fuit, vel erit, præter unum Christum, corpus suum et sanguinem in cruce Deo offerentem. . . . Christus in Eucharistiâ corporaliter non est, ut jam demonstravimus: ideoque corpus ejus ac sanguis, nisi *typice*, et per *modum commemorationis;* offerri non potest. Quare quod in Missâ realiter, et e manibus sacrifici offertur, vere ac proprie *sacrificium propitiatorium* esse non potest. 2. Sed nec omnino *verum ac proprie dictum* sacrificium in Missâ ullum est: non quale Tridentinum Concilium definivit, et vestri uno ore profitentur' ('Defensio Eccles. Angl.,' c. lxxiv., p. 536, A.C.L.).

II.

'Quid igitur? An Christi Corpus, an Ejus substantia in Missâ consumitur? An Christus (qui vivens est cum offertur) vere et realiter occiditur? An desinit id esse quod prius erat? Quam hæc *impia* et *blasphema!*' (*ibid.*, p. 537, A.C.L.).

Bishop Field.

I.

'The Fathers most ordinarily, when they make mention of the supper of the Lord, do term it a sacrifice. . . . Whereupon (by wrested and wrong interpretations) the Papists do build their sacrifice of the Mass: wherein the priest doth, as they say, offer to God the sacrifice of Christ's body and blood, *pro vivis et defunctis* . . . and as a *propitiation for sins*,' etc. ('Parasceve Paschæ,' pp. 206, 207. London, 1624).

II.

'St. Augustin saith: "*Tum immolatum fuisse Christum pro nobis, cum in Eum credimus.* . . ."

And again: "*Tum pro unoquoque mortuus est Christus, quando pro se mortuum esse illum certo persuasus est....*" So that ... the Lord's Supper is not *sacrificium*, ἱλαστικὸν, sed εὐχαριστικὸν (*ibid.*, pp. 211, 212).

III.

'Not to dwell longer upon these *sacrilegious absurdities* of the Papists' (*ibid.*, p. 218).

Dr. T. James.

'The Papists in the Council of Trent make it *a sacrifice both for the living and the dead.* Admit it be a sacrifice (which cannot be well denied, being well understood); yet *is it neither satisfactory, nor expiatory, but remorative;* so Schoepperus: that is, *not properly a sacrifice, but a memorial of a sacrifice,* so *Erasmus. Arias Montanus* giveth the reason of both: *For we do not offer that sacrifice again: but proffer, and represent it to the memory after an unbloody manner, which was offered up once in blood; a sacrifice without the matter of a sacrifice,* to speak in *Cyril's* terms. Neither will it avail the Papists to say that Melchisedec sacrificed.... Vetablus affirmeth of Melchisedec in special, that *he re-*

lieved or refreshed Abraham's men, and so sacrificed not at all' ('Manuduction,' p. 96. Oxford, 1625).

DEAN SUTCLIFFE.

I.

'Ubi de sacrificio agitur, praecipua est illa controversia, quam diximus; *Utrum Christi corpus et sanguis sub speciebus panis et vini vere et proprie Deo Patri offeratur.* Hoc ille asserunt, hoc nos voce quantum possumus maxima negamus' ('Adv. Missae Pap. Sacrificium, Lib. iii., c. i., fol. 220 *b.* London, 1603).

II.

'Hoc proprium est Christi officium, offerre Corpus et sanguinem suum, et satisfacere pro peccatis. . . . *Insaniunt* ergo sacrifici synagogae Rom. qui putant se corpus et sanguinem Christi proprie offerre. Praeterea *blasphemant,* qui se mediatores constituunt inter Deum et homines, et suis sacrificiis commentitiis peccata tolli docent' (*ibid.,* c. xi., fol. 249 *b*).

III.

'*Sine sanguinis effusione,* inquit apostolus, *non fit remissio.* . . . Respondet [Bellarminus] . . . sanguinem sub specie vini fundi, dum offertur et *donatur Deo in sacrificium.* At si sub specie alienâ fundi, sit vere fundi ; tunc sacrificium missæ erit cruentum. Si vero non vere fundatur, tunc non erit sacrificium missæ vere propitiatorium. Interim vero, observandum est, hunc modum loquendi de effusione sanguinis in aliena specie, novum esse et *absurdum.* Qua enim ratione potest sanguis fundi in aliena specie ?' (*ibid.*, c. xvi., fol. 308).

Bishop Forbes (of Edinburgh).

I.

'Quod autem ad extrahendas defunctorum animas e flammis purgatorii sacrificia missarum exiguntur, et quidem sæpe repetita ; otiosorum hominum et simplicitate populorum ad quæstum malè abutentium, commentum* est ' ('Considerationes Modestæ,' Lib. III., De Euch., § 15, vol. ii., pp. 608, 610, A.C.L.).

II.

'Quotquot Romanenses defendunt, in Missâ verè et proprè Corpus Christi sacrificari, mirum quàm ipsis aqua hæreat, et inter se pugnantibus sententiis concertent ' (*ibid.*, § 12, p. 578).

* Compare the words of King James, as quoted above, p. 108.

Bishop Lake.

I.

'The act was but once done, and that only upon the cross, but the efficacy thereof continueth for ever ... and this cutteth up the *very roots* from whence springeth *the Mass*, and all attendants thereupon' (Sermons, 'De Tempore,' p. 170. London, 1629).

II.

'The *most notorious corruption* of these words [of Institution] is, that they are made a part of the priest's ordination; as if they did give him power to sacrifice both for quick and dead; for from these words do they derive that part of the priesthood; yea, upon these words they build the Mass also, as if *Hoc facite* were as much as sacrifice, and immolate Christ unbloodily. But I will not stand to refute them' (*ibid.*, p. 175).

Bishop Lewis Bayly.

I.

'Christ never ordained in the New Testament any order of *sacrificing priests.* . . . Neither is there any real priest in the New Testament but *only Christ*' ('Practice of Piety,'* p. 614. London, 1668).

II.

'There is as much difference between such a communion [the communion of the sick] and the *anti-Christian idol* of a private Mass, as there is betwixt heaven and hell' (*ibid.*, p. 617).

BISHOP MORTON.

I.

'They believe their Mass to be a *proper visible sacrifice*, that is, *a true sacrificing of Christ Himself to His Father, though without bloodshed, by the hands of the priest: a sacrifice of itself properly propitiatory for the sins of so many, as the priest,* by his memento, *extendeth it unto*. But we, yielding the all-sufficiency of meritorious propitiation unto Christ's bodily sacrifice upon the altar of the Cross, do acknowledge that the offerture of Christ in the Eucharist is not that corporal oblation, but, according to the tenor of all ancients, a memorial and commemoration thereof. Agreeable unto the writings which our adversaries

---

* This book was dedicated to Charles, Prince of Wales, and was highly esteemed in the seventeenth century.

attribute to S. Gregory, wherein it is said that *Christ is so offered in this sacrifice, that although He die no more, yet by it He is mystically sacrificed:* expounding it thus: that *this sacrifice is an imitation of His passion:* adding that *Christ doth suffer again for us in this mystery* [" pro nobis iterum patitur "]. Christ *suffer again?* This word is more than our Romanists will maintain in the proper and literal signification, and therefore must be contented to expound that Christ is in the Eucharist, so said by S. Gregory to have been *sacrificed*, as He is said therein to have *suffered;* which is not by any corporal passion, but by a mystical representation, which will appear to have been the universal doctrine of the elder Church' ('Catholic Appeal,' Lib. I., c. ii., § 12, p. 10. London, 1610).

II.

'Lest that there might be any ambiguity, how it doth pacify God, whether by His gracious acceptance, or the efficacy of offering, your General Roman Catechism, authorized both by your Council of Trent, and the then Pope Pius V., from the direction of your whole Church, instructeth you all, concerning your sacrifice of the Mass, that, *as it is a sacrifice*, it hath *an efficacy and virtue, not only of merit, but also of satisfaction*. So they, as truly setting down the true nature of a *propitiatory sacrifice*. . . . Be it known that our Church of England, in her Thirty-first Article, saith of your propitiatory sacrifice of the Mass, as it is taught by you, that it is *a blasphemous fable, and dangerous deceit*' (Bishop Morton, 'Of the Institution of the Sacrament,' Book VI., c. viii., p. 475. London, 1635).

Meyer.

'How absurd it is to hold the sacrament of the Lord's Supper to be a sacrifice propitiatory for the quick and the dead, seeing it is only a remembrance of a sacrifice . . . and yet so impudent have some been, as that they not only affirm it to be a sacrifice, but more available than the very sacrifice of Christ upon the Cross. . . . No magnifier of the Mass durst have sung so high a note, but in a church where the true remembrance of Christ's death is so obscured and falsified by the bastard Mass' ('English Catechism Explained,' p. 519. London, 1623.* 'Published by Command').

MEDE.

I.

[The Churches of the Roman Communion] 'have for many ages disused this oblation of bread and wine, and brought in, in lieu thereof, a real Hypostatical Oblation of Christ Himself. This *blasphemous* oblation we have taken away, and justly' (Mede, 'The Christian Sacrifice,' Book II., c. viii., Works, p. 376. London, 1677).

II.

'Though the Eucharist be a sacrifice (that is, an oblation wherein the offerer banquets with God), yet is Christ in this sacrifice no otherwise offered than by way *of commemoration only* of His sacrifice once offered upon the Cross' (*ibid.*, Book II., c. ix., p. 376).

* In the fifth edition, 1635, this will be found in p. 55. This edition was 'published by command' after the accession of Archbishop Laud to the primacy. And it contains some changes which may be supposed to be due to his censorship or influence (see Goode on 'Eucharist,' vol. ii., p. 697). But no change was made in the quotation here given.

III.

'Well, then, Christ is offered in this sacred supper, not *hypostatically*, as the Papists would have Him (for so He was but once offered), but *commemoratively* only' (*ibid.*, p. 376).

Bishop Bedell.

I.

'As for the other power to sacrifice, if it be any otherwise than the celebrating the commemoration of Christ's sacrifice once offered on the Cross, it is no part of the priesthood or ministry of the New Testament, but a superstitious addition thereunto' (Burnet's 'Life of Bedell,' p. 164).

II.

'You may openly profess your not doubting of any Article of the Catholic faith . . . but that you consent not to certain opinions, which are no points of faith, which have been brought into common belief, without warrant of Scriptures, or pure antiquity, as, namely . . . that the bread in the Lord's Supper is transubstantiated into His body; that He is there sacrificed for the quick and the dead' (*ibid.*, p. 199).

III.

'If you consider well the words of the Master of the sentences ... how *that what is consecrated by the priest is called a sacrifice and oblation, because it is a memorial and representation of the true sacrifice and holy offering made on the altar of the Cross*, and join thereto that of the Apostle, that *by that one offering Christ hath perfected for ever them that are sanctified*, and as he saith in another place, *through that blood of His Cross reconciled unto God all things whether in earth or in heaven;* you shall perceive that we do offer sacrifice for the quick and dead,* remembering, representing and mystically offering that sole sacrifice for the quick and dead, by the which all their sins are meritoriously expiated, and desiring that by the same, *we and all the Church* may obtain remission *of sins, and all other benefits of Christ's* passion' (*ibid.*, p. 479).

Bishop Davenant.

'Statuunt Papistæ, hoc quod somniàrunt sacrificium, pro intentione sacerdotis offerentis posse

* See Appendix, note B.

ad quos vis homines particulares, sive vivos sive mortuos, applicari ; ita ut ex ipso opere operato consequantur remissionem à pœnis et culpis, aliaque spiritualia et temporalia beneficia. . . . Per opus autem operatum . . . posse illud vivificum sacrificium applicari . . . soli audent asserere qui frontem habent ferream ; soli possunt credere, qui cor habent plumbeum. . . . Sed tædet me *errores* tam *crassos* prolixè refellere. Concludo. . . . Missam Pontificiam non esse sacrificium propitiatorium pro vivis et mortuis, sed *fœdissimum lucri aucupium* ex vivis et mortuis ' (' Determinationes Quæstionum,' Qu. xiii., pp. 64, 65. Cambridge, 1634).

Featley.

1.

'This resemblance between them satisfieth not our adversaries; they strain this text to draw blood from it, even the blood of Christ sacrificed in the Mass. If (say they) Christ be a priest for ever after the order of Melchizedek, then He must daily offer a sacrifice unto God under the forms of bread and wine, as also did Melchizedek.

And this is the fairest evidence they bring out of Scripture for the sacrifice of the Mass. Against which we object' ('Clavis Mystica,' p. 562. London, 1636).

II.

'I demand, then, after what order our Popish priests are made? Whether after the order of Aaron or Melchizedek? If after the order of Aaron, then are they to offer bloody sacrifices, and perform other carnal rites, long ago abrogated; if after the order of Melchizedek, then they are very happy. For then they are to be kings and priests, then they are not to succeed any other, nor any other them; then, as hath been shewed, they are singular, everlasting, and royal priests' (*ibid.*, pp. 564, 565).

III.

'From idolatry in the second acception they can never clear themselves, but by changing their tenets, and reforming their practice. . . . What is Popery almost else but an addition of human traditions to God's commandments and His pure worship? What is their offering of Christ in the Mass for a propitiatory sacrifice for the living and the dead ? their elevation of the host ? . . . but religious, or rather irreligious, rites brought in by the Church without any command or warrant from God's Word ?' (*ibid.*, pp. 786, 787. London, 1636).

IV.

'It was unlawful for them (the Corinthians) to sit at the same table with idolaters when they kept their solemn feast. Can it be lawful for us to stand at the same altar with them ?' (*ibid.*, p. 796).

J. Forbes (of Corse).

I.

'Non enim in eo consistet perpetuitas Sacerdotii Christi, ut semper fiat Ejus vera immolatio, per Sacerdotes, ac si necesse esset Sacerdotium Ejus per mortem extingui, nisi fierent istæ iteratæ sacrificationes in Missis : ut *impie*, et *contra Scripturas*, tradiderunt Tridentini, sess. 22. Sed constat in perpetuo vigore illius unicæ immolationis in passione semel factæ, et perpetua intercessione pro nobis, ad dextram Patris' ('Inst. Hist. Theol.,' Lib. XI., c. xx., Op., tom. ii., p. 575. Amsterdam, 1702).

II.

'Neque opus est alia Oblatione propitiatoriâ, neque ei locus esse potest: nisi (quod cogitatu *blasphemum* est) dicatur Christum illa sui unicâ oblatione non obtinuisse æternam redemptionem credentibus' (*ibid.*, p. 571).

Bishop Griffith Williams.

'*Sacrificium* ἱλαστικόν, the propitiatory sacrifice for our sins is twofold: 1. *Cruentum*, bloody. 2. *Incruentum*, unbloody.

'First, the bloody sacrifice for our sins is that which our Saviour Christ once offered upon the altar of His Cross, to appease His Father's wrath, and to make satisfaction for the sins of the whole world.... And of this invaluable sacrifice, and of the unity, necessity, efficacy, and perpetuity of the same, the Author of the Epistle unto the Hebrews doth most excellently and abundantly treat.

'Secondly, the unbloody sacrifice for our sins is likewise twofold:

'First, the commemoration of that bloody sacrifice which Christ offered for us, which we always make, as often as we receive the sacrament of the Lord's supper; not that we offer Christ herein unto the Father, as newly tendered for our sins, for *then must He often suffer* (as the Apostle saith); but that we desire God, as often as we receive this sacrament, to accept that sacrifice which Christ hath once offered, to be a plenary satisfaction for all sins.

'Secondly, repentance for our sins. . . . Of this sacrifice the Prophet David speaketh, saying, The sacrifice of God is a troubled spirit' ('The True Church,' Lib. II., c. 15, p. 207. London, 1629).

Archbishop Laud.

I.

'As Christ offered up Himself once for all, a full and all-sufficient sacrifice for the sin of the whole world, so did He institute and command a memory of this sacrifice in a sacrament, even till His coming again. . . . It is safest for a man to believe the commemorative, the praising, and the performing sacrifice, and to offer them duly to God, and to leave the Church of Rome in this particular to her *superstitions*, that I may say *no more*' ('Conference with Fisher,' § 35, part 3, pp. 257, 258. Oxford, 1839).

II.

'By the Book of Common Prayer and Ordinations, they are called and made *presbyteri*, priests,* as appears thereby. And as touching the function of *sacrificing*, whereby, *they say, a true and proper sacrifice* is to be made for the sins of the quick and the dead, and an oblation of the very body and blood of Christ. *We say*, that forasmuch as our priests have authority to minister the sacraments, and consequently the Eucharist, which is a representation of the sacrifice of Christ; therefore they may be said to offer† Christ in a mystery, and to sacrifice Him by way of commemoration'‡ ('Objections against Lawfulness of Bishops,' c. 5, p. 48).

* So in p. 32 of the same Introduction, we have (from Hutton, see p. 26) 'The Holy Ghost giving the name πρεσβύτερος to our ministers, which in the original (whence priest is derived) gives no other name but what the Communion Book calls them by.'

† See Appendix, Note B.

‡ This is from an appendix to Dr. Nicholl's 'On the Common Prayer' (London, 1712), entitled 'An Introduction to the Liturgy of the Church of England, written by way of Preface before Archbishop Laud's Collection of Various

III.

'For the deacons assisting the priest in saying Mass and sacrificing; we hold it a profane usage, neither lawful for the priest to do nor the deacon to assist in' (*ibid.*, p. 48).

IV.

'Our Church by the Articles of 1562, Article XXXI., teacheth that the offering of Christ once made is sufficient and perfect, and that there needs no other satisfaction for sins, and consequently *condemns the Mass* for the quick and the dead as *blasphemous*. And by the place of Acts xiii. 2, there cannot be anything thence inferred to prove that their ministering at that time may warrant the Popish Massing, in these times, as now it is used' (*ibid.*, p. 48).

V.

''Tis one thing to offer up His body, and another to offer up the memorial of His body with our praise and thanks for that infinite bless-

---

Readings out of the several Ancient Common-Prayer Books.' It may probably be presumed to be expressive of the Archbishop's views, or, at least, of views which he accepted and approved.

ing; so that ... I do not see how any *Popish meaning* ... can be fastened upon it [*i.e.*, the inverting the order of the communion in the Scotch Liturgy]' ('Troubles and Trials,' p. 115. See Works, vol. iii., p. 345, A.C.L.).

VI.

'If Bellarmine ... mean, that the priest offers up that which Christ Himself did, and not a *commemoration of it only*, he is erroneous in that, and can never make it good' (*ibid.*, vol. iii., pp. 358, 359).

MONTAGUE.

'You well confess the blessed sacrament of the altar, or communion table, whether you please, to be a sacrifice. *Not propitiatory*, as they call it (I will use the word "*call it*," lest you challenge me upon Popery, for using "propitiatory") for the living and dead. Not an external, visible, true, and proper sacrifice, but only representative, remorative, and spiritual sacrifice'* ('Appeal to Cæsar,' p. 287. 1625).

---

* Waterland, referring to his 'Origines Ecclesiasticæ' and to his 'Antidiatribe,' says: 'It is certain that Bishop Montague, of that time, understood the whole *Action*, or

Vindiciæ Ecclesiæ Anglicanæ, by W. T.

'The Church of Rome hath transfigured this sacrament into a sacrifice propitiatory for the sins of the living, and of the dead. And to this end they have brought into the Church of Christ, contrary to His Word, a priest, and an altar. . . . Of offering a sacrifice propitiatory to take away our sins, and that daily, and by the priest, there is no word in the Scripture for it. Contrariwise the Scriptures teach directly the contrary, and declare this doctrine to be full of *error and blasphemy*' (p. 51. London, 1630).

Canons of 1640.

' Albeit at the time of reforming this Church from that gross superstition of Popery, it was carefully provided that all means should be used to root out of the minds of the people, both the inclination thereunto, and the memory thereof; *especially of the idolatry committed in the Mass,* for which cause all popish altars were demolished.

Memorial Service, to be a *true* and *real* sacrifice of praise ' (Works, vol. v., p. 138. Oxford, 1843).

On the subject of Montague's intercourse with Panzani see above, Introduction, pp. 28, 29.

Yet notwithstanding it was then ordered by the injunctions and advertisements of Queen Elizabeth, of blessed memory, that the holy tables should stand where the altars stood, and accordingly have been continued in the royal chapels of three famous and pious princes, and in most cathedral and some parochial churches, which doth sufficiently acquit the manner of placing the said tables from any illegality, or just suspicion of popish superstition or innovation . . . We declare that this situation of the holy table doth not imply that it is, or ought to be, esteemed *a true and proper altar*, whereon Christ is again *really sacrificed:* but it is and may be called an altar by us, in that sense in which the primitive Church called it an altar, and in *no other*' (Canon VII. See Cardwell's 'Synodalia,' vol. i., pp. 404, 405).*

* These Canons are only cited here as expressing the views of the Bishops and Clergy in Convocation of this date. For this purpose they have unquestionably much value. On the history of this Convocation see Neal's 'Hist. of Puritans,' vol. i., pp. 625 *sqq*. On the question of the authority of the Canons see Cardwell's 'Synodalia,' vol. i, pp. 380 *sqq*. The Canons were 'freely and unanimously subscribed' (see Laud's Works, vol. iii., p. 291, A.C.L., and Heylyn's 'Cyprianus Anglicus,' pp. 446. London, 1668).

Archbishop Ussher.

I.

'So it is in this ministry of the blessed sacrament; the service is first presented unto God (from which, as from a most principal part of the duty, the sacrament is called the Eucharist, because therein we offer a special sacrifice of praise and thanksgiving always unto God) and then communicated unto the use of God's people. . . . They did not distinguish the sacrifice from

---

They were afterwards subscribed by the Convocation of York.

In the same Canon is repudiated 'any opinion of a corporal presence of the body of Jesus Christ on the holy table, or in mystical elements.' The sixth Canon imposes ' the *Et Cætera* oath,' in which it is declared 'I will not endeavour by myself or any other, directly or indirectly, to bring in any popish doctrine contrary to that which is so established ; nor will I ever give my consent . . . ever to subject it [this Church] to the usurpations and superstitions of the See of Rome.'

To these Canons one Bishop refused at first to subscribe (scrupling 'some passages about the corporal Presence.' See Fuller, vol. iii., p. 409. London, 1837), and was therefore suspended by Laud. This was Goodman of Gloucester, who had been guilty of simony (see Laud's Works, vol. vii., p. 62 note, A.C.L.), and had already secretly consented to become a papist. (See Laud's Works, vol. iii., pp. 287-289, A.C.L., and Heylyn's 'Cyprianus Anglicus,' pp. 446, 447. See also Lathbury's 'Hist. of Convocation,' p. 250, and Perry's ' Hist. of Church of England,' pp. 610, 611.)

the sacrament, as the Romanists do nowadays.
. . . Whereby it doth appear that the sacrifice of the elder times was not like unto the new Mass of the Romanists, wherein the priest alone doth all, but unto our communion' ('Of the Religion Professed by the Ancient Irish,' c. iv., Works, vol. iv., pp. 277, 278. Edit. Ebrington, Dublin, 1847).

II.

'It appeareth that an honourable commemoration of the dead was herein intended, and a sacrifice of thanksgiving for their salvation rather than of propitiation for their sins' (*ibid.*, c. iii., p. 269).

III.

'The Rhemists indeed tell us that when the Church doth offer and sacrifice Christ daily, "He in mystery and sacrament dieth." Further than this they durst not go, for if they had said He died really, they should thereby not only make themselves daily killers of Christ, but also directly cross that principle of the Apostle, "Christ being raised from the dead dieth no more." If then the body of Christ in the administrations of the

Eucharist be propounded as dead (as hath been shewed)—and die it cannot really, but only in mystery and sacrament—how can it be thought to be contained under the outward element, otherwise than in sacrament and mystery? And such as in times past were said to have received the sacrifice from the hand of the priest, what other body and blood could they expect to receive therein but such as was suitable to the nature of that sacrifice, to wit, mystical and sacramental?' (*ibid.*, c. iv., Works, vol. iv., p. 282).

Bishop Hall.

I.

'That in this Sacred Supper there is a Sacrifice in that sense wherein the Fathers spake, none of us ever doubted. . . . But for any propitiatory sacrifice, unless it be, as the gloss interprets it, representatively, I find none. . . . What can either be spoken or conceived more plain than those words of God, *once offered, one Sacrifice, one Oblation?* . . . While they solemnly offer the Son of God up unto His Father, they humbly beseech Him, in a religious *blasphemy*, that He would be pleased to bless and accept that oblation. . . . We will gladly receive our Saviour, offered by Himself to His Father, and offered to us by His Father: we will not offer Him to His Father. Which one point, while we stick at, as we needs must, we are strait stricken with the thunderbolt of the Anathema of Trent' (Bishop Hall, 'No Peace with Rome,' Works, vol. ix., pp. 66, 67. London, 1808).

II.

'The contradiction of the Trent Fathers is here very remarkable. . . . They say, that Christ offered up that sacrifice then, and this now: St. Paul says He offered up that sacrifice, and no more. . . . St. Paul says, that He offered Himself but once for the sins of the people; they say, He offers Himself daily for the sins of quick and dead. And if the Apostle, in the spirit of prophecy, foresaw this error, and would purposely forestall it, he could not speak more directly, than when he saith, "We are sanctified through the offering of the body of Jesus Christ, once for all,"' etc. (Works, vol. ix., p. 259).

Bishop Prideaux (1578-1650).

'Altare Metonymicum pro Christo substituere, atque inde conficto relationis sophismate sacerdotium et sacrificium astruere, est *figmentum blasphemum* et idololatricum : sed hoc faciunt Romanenses in Missâ. . . . Christus unica oblatione in cruce consummavit in perpetuum eos qui sanctificantur, Heb. x. 14. . . . Ubi autem est *remissio* peccatorum, ibi non est *amplius oblatio*, praesertim *expiatoria* pro peccatis (*ibid.*, x. 18). Ergo aliud obtrudere sacrificium (ut fit in Missâ) est prorsus *idololatricum*' ('Fasciculus Controversiarum'; De Sacramentis, Quaest. vi., pp. 295, 296. Oxford, 1649).

Archbishop John Williams.

'The Thirty-first Article having taken away the Popish Lamb (for the which that old altar had been erected) as a *blasphemous figment and pernicious imposture;* the Homily had commanded us to take heed, we should look to find it in the blessed sacrament of the Lord's Supper, for there it was not ; there was indeed in the sacrament a memory of a sacrifice, but *sacrifice* there was none. And we must take heed of quillets and distinctions, that may bring us back again to the old error reformed in the Church. . . . Our truly learned men do set down precisely that a *commemorative sacrifice* is not *properly a sacrifice,* but (as K. James took it rightly) *commemoratio sacrificii,* a *commemoration only of a sacrifice*' ('Holy Table, Name and Thing,' pp. 102-105. 1637).

Bishop White.

I.

'The things which we simply condemn in the Popish Mass are these: 1. That Christ existing in earth, covered with forms of bread and wine, is in His very substance offered to God His Father. 2. We reject private Masses, in which the priest eateth alone, and undertaketh for a fee to apply the fruit thereof to particular persons. . . . 5. That it saveth *ex opere operato,* for temporal punishment. 6. And is beneficial to the defunct as well as to the living' ('Orthodox Faith,' Untruth 26, p. 340; see Pocklington's 'Altare Christianum,' p. 132).

II.

'The New Testament acknowledgeth no proper

sacrificing priests, but Christ Jesus only. . . . Neither is there any word or sentence in our Saviour's doctrine concerning any real sacrifice, but only of Himself upon the Cross; neither was any altar used and ordained by Christ and His Apostles. And if in all real sacrifices the matter of the oblation must be really destroyed and changed, and no physical destruction or change is made in the body of Christ, or in the elements of bread and wine by transubstantiation; then Romists have devised a real sacrifice in the New Testament, which hath no Divine institution' ('Reply to Fisher,' p. 465. London, 1624).

POCKLINGTON.

I.

'Bishop Montague, speaking (as he saith himself) in Bishop Morton's words, saith thus: "I believe no such sacrifice of the *altar*, as the Church of Rome doth. I fancy no such *altars*, as they employ, though I profess a sacrifice, and an altar. . . . It appeareth plainly from hence, that our Church doth not condemn the sacrifice of the altar, mentioned in the Holy Fathers, for blasphemous figments and dangerous deceits, but the sacrifice of Masses; because the common opinion of them was that they were propitiatory, external, visible, true and proper sacrifices for the quick and the dead. For had they been commonly held to be no more, but representative, remorative, and spiritual sacrifices, our Church would not then, doth not now, find any fault with them'" ('Altare Christianum,' pp. 130, 131. London, 1637).

II.

'To what purpose else is this confused blending and jumbling of these things (which the Vicar innocently desired) with that other oblation which the Papists were wont to offer upon their altars, but to make the simple deluded people believe that all these are alike blasphemous figments and pernicious impostures? And that the Church that now is, is become an utter enemy to that it was in '62, and altogether departed from the faith and Articles of Religion then held; therefore such priests and priesthood ought to be cast out, and their altars or tables set altar-wise, and their oblations to be had in *like abomination*, with that other oblation which the Papists were wont to offer on their altars; all which are blasphemous *figments and pernicious impostures.*" (*ibid.*, pp. 136, 137).

BIRKBEK.

'Come to another main point, the *proper* and *propitiatory sacrifice* for the quick and dead, and see whether at Luther's appearing, before and after, all that used that Liturgy had such an opinion of a sacrifice.

'St. Ambrose and St. Chrysostom, by way of correction, say, *we offer* the same *sacrifice, or rather the remembrance thereof.*

'Peter Lombard proposing the question, Whether that which the priest doth, may properly be named a sacrifice, or immolation, answereth, that *Christ was only once truly offered in sacrifice; and that He is not properly immolated or sacrificed, but in sacrament and representation only.*

'Lyra saith, that, *If thou say the sacrifice of the altar is daily offered in the Church, it must be answered, that there is no reiteration of the sacrifice, but a daily commemoration of that sacrifice that was once offered on the Cross.*

'Georgius Wicelius, a man much honoured by the Emperors Ferdinand and Maximilian, defines the Mass to be *a sacrifice rememorative, and of praise and thanksgiving, where many give thanks for the price of their redemption.*

'By that which hath been said, it is clear that the best and worthiest guides of God's Church, both before and after Luther's time, taught not any new real offering of Christ to God the Father as a propitiatory sacrifice to take away sins, but in effect as we do' ('Protest. Evidence,' Cent. xvi., p. 431. London, 1657).

FERNE.

I.

'For his *veri sacerdotes*, we say, as there are no such priests under the Gospel, so is there no need that Bishops should first be made such; for priests, in the Romish sense, are such as, in their ordination, "receive a power of sacrificing for the quick and the dead," *i.e.*, a real offering up again the Son of God to His Father' (see Tract 81, p. 154).

II.

'All this considered, we see how needless, unwarrantable, and presumptuous a thing this, their sacrifice of the Mass; and that such also is the power of sacrificing given to their priests' (*ibid.*, p. 159).

Bishop Sanderson.

I.

'If, together with this true religion of faith, repentance and obedience, they [many of our forefathers] embraced also your additions, as their blind guides then led them; prayed to our Lady, kneeled to an Image, crept to a Cross, *flocked to a Mass*, as you now do, these were their *spots* and their *blemishes*, these were their hay and their stubble, these were their *errors* and their *ignorances*. . . . And upon the same ground we have cause also to hope charitably of many thousand poor souls in Italy, Spain, and other parts of the Christian world at this day, that by the same blessed means they may obtain mercy and salvation in the end, although in the meantime, through ignorance, they defile themselves with much foul idolatry, and many gross superstitions. . . . But I do not so excuse the *idolatry* of our forefathers, as if it were not in itself a sin, and that, without repentance, damnable' (Works, vol. iii., pp. 228, 229. Oxford, 1854).

II.

'Considered formally, in regard of those points which are properly of Popery [the Church of Rome] is become a false and corrupt Church, and is indeed an Antichristian synagogue, and not a true Christian Church, taking truth in the second sense. . . . The doctrinal errors of the Church of Rome do not directly and immediately overthrow the foundation of faith, as the heresy of the Arian Churches did ; but mediately and by necessary consequence they do. As in the points of Merits, *Mass*, Transubstantiation, etc. . . . The imposing these errors upon the consciences of men, to be believed as of necessity, is damnable, and doth not only justify a separation already made, but also bindeth *sub mortali* all true Christians to such a separation' (*ibid.*, vol. v., pp. 246, 247).

HAMMOND.

I.

'The breaking and eating of the bread is a communication of the Body of Christ, a sacrifice commemorative of Christ's offering up His body for us, and a making us partakers, or commu-

nicating to us the benefits of that Bread of Life'
('Practical Catechism,' Lib. VI., § iv., Works,
vol. i., p. 129. London, 1684).

II.

'I will now give you a compendium or brief of the main substantial part of this sacrament. And that consists only of two branches, one on our parts performed to God, the other on God's part performed to us. That on our part is commemorating the goodness of God in all, but especially that His great bounty of giving His Son to die for us: and this commemoration hath two branches, one of praise and thanksgiving to Him for this mercy, the other of annunciation or showing forth, not only first to men, but secondly, and especially, to God, this sacrifice of Christ's offering up His body upon the Cross for us. That which respecteth or looks towards men, is a professing of our faith in the death of Christ; that which looks towards God, is our pleading before Him that sacrifice of His own Son, and, through that, humbly and with affiance requiring the benefits thereof, grace and pardon, to be bestowed upon us. And then God's part is the accepting of this our bounden duty, bestowing that body and blood of Christ upon us, not by sending it down locally for our bodies to feed on, but really for our souls to be strengthened and refreshed by it : as when the sun is communicated to us, the whole bulk and body of the sun is not removed out of its sphere, but the rays and beams of it, and with them the light and warmth and influences, are really and verily bestowed or darted out upon us' (*ibid.*, p. 129).

III.

'S. *The first question then is* [Why the sacrament of the Lord's Supper was ordained ?]. *And the answer* [For the continual remembrance of the sacrifice of the death of Christ, and of the benefits which we receive thereby]. *What is the meaning of that answer?*'

'C. Dissolve the words, and you shall see most clearly. First, Christ died. Secondly, this death of His was a sacrifice for us, an *oblation once for all offered* to the Father for us weak sinful men. Thirdly, by this sacrifice we that are true Christians receive unspeakable benefits ; as strength to repair our weakness, and enable us to do what God in His son will accept : and reconciliation, or pardon for us miserable sinners. And fourthly, the end of Christ's instituting this sacrament was on purpose that we might, at set times, frequently and constantly returning (for this is the meaning of *continual*, parallel to the use of [without ceasing] applied to the sacrifice among the Jews, and the duty of prayer among Christians) remember and commemorate before God and man this sacrifice of the death of Christ' (*ibid.*, p. 130).

IV.

' He omits the two principal [controversies] concerning their private Masses, and denying the cup, their no-communion and their half-communion. . . . 'Tis visible that the Protestants of the Church of England believe and reverence, as much as any, the sacrifice of the Eucharist, as the most substantial and essential act of our religion ; and doubt not but the word *Missa*, "Mass," has fitly been used by the Western Church to signify it ; and herein *abhor and condemn* nothing, but the *corruptions and mutilations* which the Church of Rome, without care of conforming themselves to the Universal, have admitted in the celebration' (Preface to 'Dispatcher Dispatched,' quoted from No. 81 of 'Tracts for the Times,' p. 165).

HEYLYN.

I.

'Which sacrifice he [Bishop Andrewes] sometimes calls *commemorationem sacrificii*, and sometimes *sacrificium commemorativum*, a *commemorative sacrifice*. The like we find in Bishop Morton, who in his book of the "Roman Sacrifice," l. 6, c. 5, called the Eucharist a *representative* and *commemorative sacrifice*, in as plain terms as can be spoken. But what need anything have been said for the proof hereof, when the most Reverend Archbishop Cranmer, one (and the chief) of the compilers of the public liturgy, and one who suffered death for opposing the sacrifice of the Mass, distinguisheth most plainly between the sacrifice propitiatory, made by Christ Himself only, and the sacrifice commemorative and gratulatory, made by priests and people?' (Cyprianus Anglicus,' p. 23.)

II.

'When by the Articles of Religion agreed upon in Convocation, Anno 1562, the sacrifice of the Mass was declared to be *a pernicious imposture, a blasphemous figment*, and that transubstantiation was declared to be repugnant to the plain words of Holy Scripture, to overthrow the nature of a sacrament, and to have given occasion to many superstitions : yet still the doctrine of a real presence* was maintained as formerly ' (*ibid.*, p. 24).

III.

' The Article . . . determineth positively that the sacrifice of Masses, *in the which it was commonly said that the priests did offer Christ for the quick and the dead, to have remission of pain or guilt, were blasphemous fables, and pernicious deceits*. And therefore had the Vicar of Gr. erected or intended to erect an altar for such a sacrifice, he had not only sacrificed his discretion on it, but also his religion ; and been *no longer worthy to be called a son of the Church of England*' ('Coal from the Altar,' § 1, p. 7. London, 1636).

The context following makes it clear that the phrase 'Real Presence' is used in the Reformed sense. See 'Theology of Bishop Andrewes,' pp. 9-17, and 'Real Presence of the Laudian Theology,' pp. 55-58.

IV.

'We may speak in proper and significant terms, as the Fathers did, *without approving* either the *Popish Mass* or the Jewish sacrifice. . . . Two ways there are by which the Church declares herself in the present business. . . . First, in the Articles (Article XXXI.), " The offering of Christ once made," etc. This sacrifice or oblation, once for ever made, and never more to be repeated, was by our Saviour's own appointment to be commemorated and represented to us, for the better quickening of our faith : whereof, if there be nothing said in the Book of Articles, it is because the Articles related chiefly unto points in controversy ' (*ibid.*, pp. 26, 28).

V.

' Of any *expiatory sacrifice*, of any offering up of Christ for the quick and dead, more than what had been done by Him once, and once for all, those blessed ages never dreamt. . . . They meant nothing less than to give any opportunity to the future ages of making that an *expiatory sacrifice*, which they did only teach to be *com-*

memorative, or *representative* of our Saviour's passion' ('Antidotum Lincolniense,' § 2, c. v., p. 24. London, 1637).

Bishop Gauden.

I.

'To tell you further, how undigestible to sober Christians (because *Preter-Scriptural* and *Anti-Scriptural*) the Roman practice and opinion is . . . Add to these, their profitable and popular imaginations of *Purgatory*, they applying not only prayers, but *Masses and Oblations* . . . to those that are *dead* as well as to the *living*' ('Ecclesiæ Anglicanæ Suspiria,' Book III., c. xvi., p. 309. London, 1659).

II.

'As for the English Liturgies symbolizing with the Popish Missal . . . it doth no more, than our Communion or Lord's Supper celebrated in England, doth with the *Mass* at Rome; or our doctrine about the Eucharist doth with theirs about Transubstantiation. . . . In all which particulars, how much the Church of England differed both in doctrine and devotion from that of Rome, no man that is intelligent and honest can either deny or dissemble. I am sure we differ as much as English doth from Latin, truth from error, true antiquity from novelty, completeness from defect, sanctity from sacrilege . . . as much as Divine faith doth from human fancy' (*ibid.*, Book I., c. xii., p. 88).

III.

'Contrary to which [that word of God], some of their tenets, injunctions, and practices, seem to us either to rob God of His peculiar honour . . . or to rob Christ of the glory of His only merit, mediation, satisfaction, and intercession for us' (*ibid.*, Book III., c. xv., p. 305).

Archbishop Bramhall.

1.

'For any other sacrifice, distinct from that which is propitiatory, meritorious, and satisfactory, by its own proper virtue and power, the Scriptures do not authorize, the fathers did not believe, the Protestants do not receive any such. This is a certain truth, that the passion of Christ is the only ransom and propitiation for sin' (Works, vol. v., p. 213, A.C.L.; see also p. 188, and vol. i., p. 54).

II.

'Let him that dare go one step further than we do; and say that it is a suppletory sacrifice, to supply the defects of the Sacrifice of the Cross' (*ibid.*, vol. ii., p. 276).

III.

'We have a meritorious sacrifice, that is, the Sacrifice of the Cross; we have a commemorative and applicative sacrifice, or a commemoration and application of that sacrifice, in the Holy Eucharist. A suppletory sacrifice, to supply any want or defects in that sacrifice, he dare not own; and unless he do own it, he saith no more than we say' (*ibid.*, p. 642).

IV.

'He cannot go one step further than we do in that cause without tumbling into *direct blasphemy*' (*ibid.*, p. 582). 'I have challenged them to go one step further into it than I do, and they dare not ; or, rather, they *cannot without blasphemy*' (*ibid.*, p. 633).

v.

'They are not the Protestants then, but the Romanists, who *pare off the pith of Christ's heavenly priesthood*, who daily make as many distinct propitiatory sacrifices as there are Masses in the world' (Works, vol. v., p. 220, A.C.L.).

vi.

'The Protestants dare not say that the holy Eucharist is a sacrifice propitiatory in itself, by its own proper virtue and expiatory efficacy' (*ibid.*, p. 221).

J. ELIS.

[Blasphema figmenta, et perniciosæ fuerunt imposturæ.]

'*Objicitur.* Oblationem Christi factam in cruce, repraesentandam esse in cœnâ.

'*Resp.* Oblatio Christi cruenta repræsentanda est, non per aliam oblationen incruentam, sed per panis fractionem et vini effusionem.

'*Objicitur. Missam esse sacrificii Christi applicationem.*

'*Resp.* Sacrificium Christi sola fide applicatur.

'*Objicitur. Prophetas prædixisse sacrificium futurum esse in Ecclesia,* Mal. i. 11 : Esa. lxvi. 23.

'*Resp.* Sacrificia Ecclesiæ Novi Testamenti, sunt Eucharistica, et Spiritualia, quæ duratura sunt.

'*Objicitur. Christum dixisse,* Hoc facite in Mei commemorationem, *id est, hoc sacrificate.* . . .

'*Resp.* . . . *facere* autem hoc loco non significat sacrificare, quia refertur ad actiones Christi, de quibus non proprie dicitur, quod sunt sacrificandæ' (Art. XXXIX. ; 'Eccl. Angl. Defensio,' pp. 110, 112. Amstelod., 1700).

L'Estrange.

'"*Here we offer and present,*" *etc.* This high and eminent place looketh big upon all those false clamours that our service is extracted from the Mass, challenging the authors thereof to exhibit where it is found in the canon of the Mass. No, to the utter shame of the Romish party, our Church upbraideth them, that whereas they contend so much for the propriety of the sacrifice of their Mass, the whole canon of that Mass hath not one syllable of this most proper sacrifice, this ἀμέριστος θυσία, " indivisible sacrifice," of both bodies and souls, a sacrifice enjoined by Apostolical precept (Rom. xii. 1); and which did, in the primitive times, constitute an illustrious part of the Eucharistical office' ('Alliance of Divine Offices,' p. 325. Edit. A.C.L.).

Bishop Wren.

I.

'He saith, that he was ever so far from having any thought or intention of resembling the popish manner of altars, that he believeth that he never did, by any words of his own, so much as name the word altar in any of his articles or directions' ('Parentalia,' p. 76).

II.

'In the popish Church the use is, that the priest after consecration, elevating the bread and the chalice, does it so as not to be seen over his shoulders only, but holds it up over his head, meaning that then he does sacrifice Christ's Body, which there he hath transubstantiated, and therefore to that end elevates it, that the people beholding may fall down and adore it : this defendant is ready, according to the decisions in such cases used in ancient councils, to pronounce *Anathema* to any superstitious or idolatrous usages, or intentions by him in that kind ever had, and to profess that he doth faithfully and totally adhere to the Article of the Church of England' (*ibid.*, p. 104).

Bishop Jeremy Taylor.

1.

'Christ is but once immolated or sacrificed in Himself, but every day in the sacrament; that properly, this in figure; that in substance, this in similitude; that naturally, this sacramentally and spiritually. But therefore we call this mystery a sacrifice, as we call the sacrament Christ's body, viz., by way of similitude or after a certain manner, for upon this account the names of the things are imputed to their very figures. This is St. Austin's sense, which indeed he frequently so expresses' ('Of Transubstantiation,' § 3, Works, vol. vi., p. 590. Edit. Eden).

II.

'Be sure we think as ill of your errors as you can suppose of our Articles' ('Letter to a Gentlewoman,' *ibid.*, p. 658).

Bishop Hacket.

I.

'We have no real and external sacrifice of Christ's body and blood; by Himself He did once offer a full, perfect, and sufficient sacrifice for the sins of the whole world; therefore to erect a real altar without a figurative construction is *to overthrow the Cross of Christ*. . . . Our own Church, since it renounced the opinion of an external propitiatory sacrifice in the Mass, yet in the first Liturgies, set forth by public authority in the reign of Edward VI., the name of altar is throughout retained, to comply with the figurative phrase of good antiquity; and the next edition of Liturgies, to keep an wholesome form of words, as St. Paul says, and to give no place to misconstruction, doth everywhere throughout call it the Lord's table. . . . We *neither dare nor will speak* after the sense of the Roman novelty. . . . These are not times to offer sacrifice . . . but only to commemorate that sacrifice, after which all true sacrifices ceased, and all properly-called altars fell to the ground' ('Century of Sermons,' pp. 791, 792. London, 1675).

II.

'The alteration of words [table for altar] came in . . . partly to give this evidence among others, that we had renounced the sacrifice of the Mass, the very offering up of our Saviour in an unbloody oblation, not again, but by one and the same act with which He offered up Himself on the Cross, a *chymæra* which is not intelligible to any mortal man. . . . This was our Bishop's mind; and, I take it, the same was and is in all our learned men, that in that holy sacrament there is a spectacle of the sacrifice of Christ's Body, as it suffered on the Cross, represented by breaking the bread, and pouring out the wine, by eating the one and drinking the other; that there is a commemoration of that sacrifice in the repetition of the words of institution; that there is an application of that sacrifice to their souls, that partake by faith; and that all this makes properly a sacrament, improperly and figuratively a sacrifice' ('Memorial of Archbishop Williams,' Part II., p. 106. London, 1693).

Bishop Nicholson.

I.

'It must be the Son of God only that must be the sacrifice, or else there could be no satisfaction. His blood the price, or else nothing bought; His life the ransom, or else nothing redeemed. But this sacrifice being offered, His blood being shed, His life laid down, then there was λυτρὸν, a full ransom; then there was ἀντίλυτρον, a sufficient commutation; then there was ἱλασμος, a pacification made for the sins of the whole world. His person was the only sacrifice that God would accept; His blood the only price that God would esteem; His death the sole ransom that God would receive for the transgressors' ('Exposition of the Catechism,' pp. 212, 213. Oxford, 1865).

II.

'In the flesh sin was condemned . . . by the sacrifice of Himself once offered' (*ibid.*, p. 213).

III.

'Both must be conceived with his proper attribute; the body with crucifixion, the blood with effusion; the body as given for us, the blood as shed for us. Without which reflexion they will have little comfort and heart in them. Christ's flesh and blood are the true causes of eternal life, which yet they are not by the bare force of their own substance, but through the dignity and worth of His person, which offered them up by way of sacrifice, for the life of the whole world; of which sacrifice we have in this sacrament a lively representation and memorial' (*ibid.*, p. 221; see also pp. 218, 220).

Bishop Cosin.

I.

'Christ can be no more offered, as the doctors and priests of the Roman party fancy Him to be, and vainly think that every time they say Mass they offer up and sacrifice Christ anew, as properly and truly as He offered up Himself in His sacrifice upon the Cross. And this is one of the points of doctrine, and the chief one whereof the popish Mass consisteth, abrogated, and reformed here by the Church of England, according to the express word of God' (Bishop Cosin, 'Notes on P. B.,' 2nd Series, Works, vol. v., p. 333, A.C.L.).

II.

'A true, real, proper, and propitiatory sacrificing of Christ ... which is the popish doctrine ... we hold not, believing it to be a *false* and *blasphemous* doctrine' (*ibid.*, p. 336).

III.

'A power to consecrate the sacrament, and to make a memorial of the sacrifice, we grant him : a power to transubstantiate, and really to sacrifice Christ upon the altar for the quick and the dead, we shall never grant him, that being a new doctrine which the Catholic Church never taught us' (Works, A.C.L., vol. iv., pp. 277, 278).

IV.

'There is no example of Christ followed, if your priests have a power (as truly they have none) given them to offer Christ's body in the Mass, as a real and propitiatory sacrifice to God the Father' (*ibid.*, p. 280).

V.

'As concerning their pretended power of really sacrificing the true body of Christ for the quick and the dead, there was never yet priest that had it, but Himself, nor shall ever have it to the world's end' (*ibid.*, p. 280).

VI.

'That there be any such in the Church of England (unless they be in it, and are not of it) who believe our Saviour hath left to His priests any such power of real sacrificing His body, etc., I am sure Dr. C. believes not' (*ibid.*, p. 284).

VII.

'The word *Missa*, as it is used at present among the papists, for a true and proper sacrifice of Christ offered in every celebration for the living and the dead is never used among the ancients. And for this reason the name of *Missa* or *Mass* is rejected by the Church of England, which having exploded the opinion of the sacrifice of the Mass, does disclaim the use of the word Missa in modern, though not in the ancient sense' (*ibid.*, vol. v., pp. 301, 302).

VIII.

'I told him [the prior of the English Benedictines] that (excluding their pretended and vain sense of transubstantiating the bread and wine, of a *true* and *proper altar*, and of a *real sacrificing* of the body of Christ: all which WE REJECTED as *unsound* and *uncatholic doctrine*) we had . . . a power to offer the sacrifice of the Eucharist, which is a sacrifice of praise and thanksgiving, made in the name of the Church, *for* the sacrifice that Christ made of Himself, and offered upon the altar of His cross once for all' (*ibid.*, vol. iv., p. 247).

IX.

'No one is so blind, as not to see the difference between a "proper offering," which was once performed by His death upon the Cross, and between an "improper offering" which is now made either in heaven, by that His appearance on our behalf, or here on earth, by prayers and representation, or obtestation, or commemoration, there being only the same common name for these, but a very wide difference in the things themselves' (quoted from Vogan's 'True Doctrine,' p. 455).

Dr. Isaac Barrow.

'The nature of the Lord's Supper doth imply communion and company; but they forbid any man to say that a priest may not communicate alone; so establishing the belief of nonsense and contradiction.

'The Holy Scripture teacheth us that our Lord hath departed, and is absent from us in body. . . . But the Pope with his Lateran and Tridentine Complices draw Him down from heaven, and make Him corporally present every day, in numberless places here. . . . The Scripture teacheth that our Lord was once offered for expiation of our sins; but they pretend every day to offer Him up as *a propitiatory sacrifice*. These devices without other foundation than a figurative expression . . . they with all violence and fierceness obtrude upon the belief as one of the most necessary and fundamental articles of the Christian religion' (' On Pope's Supremacy,' pp. 285, 286. London, 1683).

THORNDIKE.

I.

'The Council of Trent enjoineth to believe that Christ instituted a new passover to be sacrificed as well as represented, commemorated and offered in the Eucharist, *de Sacrificio Missæ*, Cap. 1, *which is false*' (see Tract lxxxi., p. 180).

II.

'Though the fathers divers times call the celebrating of the Eucharist the death and passion of our Lord, which it commemorates, and the sacrifice of His Cross. . . . Yet the addition of the words which they use, of "reasonable," and "unbloody," of "commemorative," of "symbolical," of "sign," and "image," are necessary evidence of an abatement in the property of the words according to their meaning' ('Laws of the Church,' ch. v., § 32, Works, vol. iv., par. i., pp. 126, 127, A.C.L.).

III.

'It is well enough known, what pretences have been made, and what consequences drawn, from the speculation of the sacrifice of Christ upon the Cross repeated or represented by this sacrament to persuade Christendom that the benefit thereof in remission of sins and infusion of grace and all the effects of Christ's passion is derived upon God's people by virtue of the mere act of assisting at the sacrifice, which hath been called *opus operatum*, or the very external work done, without consideration, without knowledge, without any intention of doing that which he is to do in it; that is, of concurring every one for his share to the doing of the same: supposing always, that this sacrifice consists in substituting the body and blood of Christ to be bodily present under the accidents of the elements, the substance of them being abolished and ceasing to be there any more; and not in offering and presenting the sacrifice of Christ crucified, here now represented by this sacrament, unto God, for obtaining the benefits of His passion in behalf of His Church' (*ibid.*, ch. xxiv., § 11, vol. iv., par. ii., p. 567).

Bishop Reynolds.

'The papists, that they may have something to build the idolatry of their Mass upon, make Melchizedek to sacrifice bread and wine, as a type of the Eucharist. . . . The priesthood of Melchizedek as type, and of Christ as the substance, was ἀπαραβατὸς, a priesthood, which could not pass unto any other . . . but the papists make themselves priests, by human and ecclesiastical ordination, to offer that which (they say) Melchizedek offered . . . and so most sacrilegiously rob Him of that honour, which He hath assumed to Himself as His peculiar office' (Explication of Ps. CX., Works, vol. ii., pp. 412, 413. London, 1826).

Bishop Laney.

'For the sacrifice . . . it is, I confess, a word of offence, because there goes under the name of a Christian sacrifice, that which our Church calls a *blasphemous fable* and *dangerous deceit*. . . . That which the Article speaks of is the sacrifice of the Mass, wherein the priests of that sacrifice say, *That Christ Himself is really sacrificed for the quick and dead'* ('Two Sermons Preached at Whitehall,' pp. 1, 2. London, 1668).

SCRIVINER.

'The question . . . must be stated concerning the sacrifice . . . whether it really and properly be predicated of the matter of the sacrament: and that in as proper a sense as Christ's body was offered upon the Cross: this *we deny* . . . Thus is the Host a sacrifice, but not essentially as the sacrifices of the law, or Christ's offering Himself; but analogically and metonymically, by virtue of the sacrifice of Christ' (quoted from Tract lxxxi., pp. 205, 206).

ARCHBISHOP LEIGHTON.

'The priesthood of the law represented Him as the Great High Priest, that *offered up Himself for our sins*, and that is altogether incommunicable; neither is there any peculiar office of priesthood for offering sacrifice in the Christian Church, but His alone who is Head of it. But this dignity that is here mentioned of a spiritual priesthood, offering spiritual sacrifices, is common to all those that are in Christ' ('On First Ep. of Peter, ch. ii., verses 4, 5,' Works, vol. i., p. 231. London, 1818).

Bishop Sparrow.

I.

'This done [*i.e.*, the reception and the saying the Lord's Prayer] the priest offers up the sacrifice of the holy Eucharist, or the sacrifice of praise and thanksgiving for the whole Church, as in all old Liturgies is appointed: and together with that is offered up that most acceptable sacrifice of ourselves, souls and bodies, devoted to God's service' ('Rationale on Common Prayer,' Part IV., pp. 180, 181. London, 1722).

II.

'Showing forth and commemorating the Lord's death, and offering upon it [the altar] the same sacrifice that was offered upon the Cross, or *rather the commemoration of that sacrifice*, St. Chrysostom in Heb. x. 9' (*ibid.*, p. 243).

III.

'But how shall the people be able to know which truths are so generally delivered from the *first ages till now?* . . . I answer, you may find and know these necessary truths, *by the public doctrine of our own Church, delivered in her* Liturgy and Articles of religion, *by the unanimous consent of all your spiritual guides.* Acquaint yourselves throughly with that public doctrine, and adhere to that; and if your own teacher teaches otherwise, believe him not' ('Caution against False Doctrines,' *ibid.*, p. 295).

Bishop Morley.

I.

'Quod vero dicit in præcedenti Capite *sacrificium pretii nostri pro eâ* [Monica] *post mortem oblatum* esse, intelligi non potest ac si offerretur pro expiatione peccatorum ejus, utpote quæ jam (ut ipse dicit) credebatur expiata ; sed ut inter offerendum memoria ejus fieret inter alios qui *in Domino* in fide Dominici Sacrificii pro peccatis expiandis, obdormierunt. . . . Adeo ut supposita hac consuetudine *pro defunctis orandi et offerendi*, in hoc sensu a veteribus usurpatâ, nihil inde auctoramenti aut argumenti pro hodiernis *Missis precibusque pro mortuis*, in *Pontificiorum* sensu celebratis, possit colligi' ('Epistolaris Dissertatio,' pp. 17, 18. London, 1683).

II.

'That which was not lawful and counted a profanation of this holy mystery in the primitive Church, is now in the Romish not only counted lawful but meritorious; I mean the standing by, and looking on the celebration of the *Lord's Supper* or the *Mass* (as they call it) without receiving of it' ('Vindication of Argument from Sense,' p. 18. London, 1683).

CUDWORTH.

I.

'This I think is the case of that *grand error* of the papists concerning the Lord's Supper being a sacrifice; which perhaps at first did rise by degeneration of a primitive truth, whereof the very obliquity of this error yet may bear some dark and obscure intimation' ('True Notion of Lord's Supper,' Introduction, p. 2. London, 1676).

II.

'We see then how that theological controversy which hath cost so many disputes, whether the Lord's Supper be a sacrifice, is already decided: for it is ... not ... *oblatio sacrificii*, but, as Tertullian excellently speaks, *Participatio sacrificii* . . . Therefore, keeping the same analogy, he [St. Paul] must needs call the communion-table by the name of the Lord's table, *i.e.*, the table upon which God's meat is eaten ; not His altar, upon which it is offered. . . . There is a sacrifice in the Lord's Supper symbolically, but not there as offered up to God, but feasted on by us ; and so not a sacrifice, but a sacrificial feast : which began too soon to be misunderstood' (*ibid.*, ch. v., pp. 27, 28).

Dr. T. Puller.

I.

'Nor doth our Church hold any true propitiatory sacrifice for dead, or living, to be offered up in the Mass ; because that would derogate from the sufficiency of Christ's priesthood ; neither doth it define its priesthood by the action only of such a sacrifice, as doth the Council of Trent' ('Moderation of the Church of England,' pp. 196, 197. Edit. Eden. London, 1870).

II.

'So exceedingly moderate and prudent was the Church, that in the seventh Canon, 1640, it abundantly cautions, lest those words [*priest* and *altar*] be used otherwise than in a *metaphorical* and *improper* attribution'* (*ibid.*, p. 172).

Towerson.

'Let us go on to inquire . . . whether he who administers this sacrament is obliged by the words of the institution or otherwise, to make an " offering to God of Christ's body and blood," . . . the Council of Trent, as is well known, avowing that to be the importance of the words, " Do this in remembrance of Me "; and that the Apostles were, by the same words, appointed priests to offer them. . . . So little is there in the words themselves, how favourably soever considered, to oblige us to understand them of such an offering as the Church of Rome advanceth. And we shall find them to signify as little, though we take in the sense of the Catholic Church upon them. . . . Which [quotation from Justin Martyr] shows him not to

---

* In the same page Puller quotes from Rivet: 'In Liturgiâ Anglicana habemus quidem sacrificii nomen, offerendi nomen, etiam hostiæ mentionem, sed nihil magis adversatur Missatico sacrificio quam tota hæc oratio.'

have thought in the least of our being commanded to offer Christ's body and blood, under the species of bread, or indeed of any other sacrifice, than a commemorative or Eucharistical one' ('Explication of Catechism,' Part IV., pp. 274, 276, 277).

Barbon.

'The word *Priest* is not *Jewish*, for Priest is the English of *Presbyter*, and not of *Sacerdos*, there being, in our tongue, no word in use for *Sacerdos*; *Priest*, which we use for *both*, being improperly used for a *Sacrificer*, as *Sacerdos* signifies, but naturally expressing a *Presbyter*, the name whereby the *Apostles* call themselves, and those which succeed them, in their charge ... Concerning the word *sacrifice*, Bishop Andrewes accounts it an imagination or fancy to take umbrage at the word. ... I aver that even *missa* or *mass* is not Popish (far ancienter than Popery), it signifying antiently, the worship of God' ('Λειτουργία θειοτέρα ἐργία,' pp. 65, 66. Oxford, 1662).

Archbishop Tillotson.

'The next instance is *the repetition of Christ's Propitiatory Sacrifice in the Mass*, so often as that is celebrated. ... It is directly contrary to the main scope of a great part of this Epistle to the Hebrews. ... There cannot be plainer texts for anything in the Bible than that this propitiatory sacrifice was never to be repeated. And whereas they say that the *sacrifice of the Mass is an unbloody sacrifice;* this, instead of bringing them off, doth but entangle the matter more. For if blood be offered in the sacrifice of the Mass, how is it an unbloody sacrifice? What can be more bloody than blood? And if blood be not offered, how is it propitiatory? Since the Apostle lays it down for a certain rule, that *without shedding of blood there is no remission* of sins, *i.e.*, there can be no propitiation for the sins of the living or the dead, which the Church of Rome affirms there is' (Works, vol. i., p. 42. London, 1712).

KETTLEWELL.

I.

' *Question.*—If the death and sacrifice of Christ were so full a satisfaction at first, there is no more now to be paid, and it need never be repeated?

'*Answer.*—No, nor ever must it. The Jewish sacrifices needed constantly to be repeated, because being of little worth, and very imperfect, their virtue was soon spent, so that *year by year they were continually offered*. . . . But His, being full and perfect from the first, and leaving nothing to be added, *He is not to be offered often, but at once hath He put away sin by the sacrifice of Himself.* But although His sacrifice is no more to be really acted, as it needs not, the whole effect of it being as fresh and full now as it was at first; yet is it daily still commemorated, and the virtue thereof applied, in every good prayer, but especially in every sacrament' (Works, vol. i., p. 612. London, 1719).

II.

'There can be no receiving of the Sacrament, without worshipping it, in the Church of Rome. . . . And these are such hindrances of communicating with that Church in *the Mass*, which are not to be urged in bar of communion, under all immoral mixtures of worship and devotions' (*ibid.*, vol. ii., p. 648).

Payne.

'The sacrifice of the Mass . . . is the great lake into which most of the Popish errors empty themselves. . . . The Mass-sacrifice contains in it a whole legion of errors, but it is only the principal one which I have endeavoured by this discourse to cast out, and that is, its being a proper and truly propitiatory sacrifice, which I have shown to be founded upon two monstrous errors, to have no true foundation in Scripture, nor no just claim to antiquity, but to be plainly contrary to both these, and to be in itself very absurd and unreasonable ' (in Gibson's ' Preservative,' vol. vi., pp. 291, 292. London, 1848).

Horneck.

I.

' The Church of Rome at this day makes strange work with consecration of the elements in the Supper of the Lord ' (' Crucified Jesus,' p. 93. London, 1727).

II.

' As the word "Eucharist" imports praise, so thanksgiving is one of the principal actions and offices in this sacrament. The Church of Rome will have it called a *sacrifice*, because in the primitive Church it went by that name. We deny it not, but then they meant by it a sacrifice of praise, and this sacrifice we exhort every one of you to offer' (*ibid.*, p. 103).

Dean Brevint.

I.

'St. Chrysostom is full and eloquent to this purpose . . . *to be offered more than once is an evidence of weakness against the oblation itself*, etc. So Roman Mass is a reproach to the infinite value of Christ's oblation, being visibly grounded on this plain *blasphemy*, that Christ's oblation on the Cross was defective' ('Roman Mass,' p. 40. Oxford, 1673).

II.

'How could the Apostle, with any either discretion or candour, absolutely deny that Christ was ever offered more than once, reserving in his own breast these limitations which no man could have guessed at, viz., *in his own shape*, or with effusion of blood, or *to redeem*, if he be as *really* offered every day a thousand times at Mass ?' (*ibid.*, pp. 37, 38).

III.

' It appears by these impieties, thus generally diffused through all the veins of Roman worship, how far that Church is a true Church. And to this purpose I advise all, whosoever will not be seduced with vain words and empty titles, to lay by what Rome hath been heretofore, and then impartially to look into what she is in these present times. And lest they should reject a Church for some particular abuse (which were not better than to cut off a tree because of some few withered leaves), let them look into what Rome is, by what *Mass* is, which is no *leaf*, or *branch*, but the main *stem* and *bulk* of that *tree*' (*ibid.*, pp. 243, 244).

IV.

' Christians before the Sacrament offered their gifts, and after it offered their prayers, their praises, and themselves. And this was the constant and solemn oblation of the Church until dark and stupid ages, which by degrees have hatched transubstantiation in the bosom of the Roman Church, have at last improved it to this *horrid direful service*, which mainly aims at this, to offer upon an altar not the bread and wine as before, but the very Body and Blood of Christ' (*ibid.*, c. vi., pp. 57, 58. Oxford, 1673).

STILLINGFLEET.

I.

' I do not think any two or three men, though never so learned, make the Church of England; her sense is to be seen in the public acts and offices belonging to it. And in the Articles ... your sacrifices on the altar are called *Blasphemous Figments and Dangerous Impostures*' (Works, vol. vi., p. 179. London, 1710).

II.

' But suppose the Son of God were to be made a true and proper sacrifice for sins on the altar, how comes it into your hands to offer Him up to the Father, since the great sacrifice of propitiation was not to be offered by any ordinary priests, but by the high priest himself, who was to carry the blood into the Holy of Holies, and there to make intercession for the people? Are you the high priests of the Gospel, to offer unto God the great sacrifice of Atonement? Is not the great High Priest of our profession entered within the veil, and is there making intercession, by virtue of His sacrifice on the Cross? What need, then, of your offering Him up again for propitiation, who offered Himself once on the Cross for a full, perfect, and sufficient sacrifice, oblation, and satisfaction for the sins of the whole world? We have all the reason in the world to commemorate, with great thankfulness and devotion, that invaluable sacrifice of the Cross; and if you will call the whole Eucharistical office a commemorative sacrifice, as the ancients did, I shall never quarrel with you about it. But how the sacrifice of the Mass comes to be propitiatory, as the sacrifice on the Cross was, I understand not; nor how it should be the same with the sacrifice of the Cross, and yet of so much less value than it, the one being said by you to be infinite, and the other finite; nor how the destruction of His sacramental, and of His natural being, should be the same thing; nor how this sacrifice should be propitiatory only for one sort of sins, and not for another; nor how the Son of God can be made a true and proper sacrifice for sin, under the species of bread and wine; nor what consumptive change that is in Him which, according to yourselves, is necessary to make Him a sacrifice. Is He slain again in the Mass? If He be, I can tell who is the Judas that betrays Him, and who are the Jews that crucify Him. If not, how comes a propitiatory sacrifice, without shedding of blood? If the consumptive change be only in the elements, then the elements are sacrificed, and not Christ. If it be only a sacramental change, what is that to a sacrifice of propitiation? And suppose all the other absurdities to be removed, and that the sacrifice of the Mass is a true, real, proper, and propitiatory sacrifice of the Son of God, body and soul, upon the altar, yet how at last comes this to be giving God thanks for the graces of His saints? I thought such a sacrifice had been much rather for the expiation of their sins' ('Conferences concerning the Idolatry of the Church of Rome,' Works, vol. vi., p. 176).

Ellis.

'Here is in this Sacrament no sacrificing of Christ, but a solemn commemoration of His sacrifice by this sacred rite commanded to be made in His Church. We do not herein, as is pretended to be done in the Romish Church, *and in their Mass*, offer up our Saviour a *propitiatory sacrifice* for the quick and dead. We only, according to Christ's own institution, commemorate that sacrifice which He Himself once offered for sin. . . . He was once offered to bear the sins of many. . . . That idol, therefore, of the papists, which the Church of Rome persuades the people so much to confide in and to pay so dear for, is a mere nothing. *It is a vain and impious fiction* to bring the priests into veneration with the ignorant and blindfolded people, who are taught to believe that a Mass-priest by muttering three or four Latin words can turn bread into God, and then can sacrifice Him again, and by devouring the whole sacrifice himself obtain remission of sins both for the quick and dead. O bless God . . . that you may not be . . . taught to believe such *blasphemous absurdities* as these' ('Scripture Catechist,' pp. 435, 436. London, 1738).

Bishop Kidder.

'What our Church holds is best learned from her declaration in her Articles. . . . She declares against "the sacrifices of Masses, in which," etc. . . . Whence it is evident that she rejects the doctrine of the Trent Council that the sacrifice of the Mass is a true and proper sacrifice propitiatory for the quick and dead. This we deny' (in Gibson's 'Preservative,' vol. vi., p. 296. London, 1848).

Bishop Patrick.

I.

'The Church of Rome binds all her members, under pain of eternal damnation, to believe both that the very same body and the very same blood which were once offered by Christ upon the Cross are daily offered up to God by the Mass-priest, and likewise (as if this were not enough) that every such offering made by the priest is a propitiatory sacrifice—nay, makes atonement as well for the dead as for the living'

(Sermon XV., Works, vol. viii., p. 244. Oxford, 1858).

II.

'This might serve for a short confutation of the sacrifices of the Mass, as they are commonly called; but that you may see that our Church was not rash in that sentence it hath pronounced against these sacrifices, as "*blasphemous fables, and dangerous deceits*," I shall a little more distinctly unfold how contradictory they are to the doctrine of the Apostle' (*ibid.*, p. 245).

III.

'There are no such priests in the Church as can offer propitiatory sacrifices to God, for this belongs to Christ alone, who is the sole priest of the New Testament. . . . It is directly against Christ's order—nay, against His office—for any man to go about to offer a proper sacrifice for sin' (*ibid.*, p. 246).

Bishop Bull.

'This proposition ["that in the Mass there is offered to God a true, proper, and propitiatory sacrifice for the living and the dead"] having that other of the " substantial presence of the body and blood of Christ in the Eucharist" immediately annexed to it, the meaning of it must necessarily be this—that in the Eucharist the very body and blood of Christ are again offered up to God as a propitiatory sacrifice for the sins of men. Which is an *impious* proposition, derogatory to the one full satisfaction of Christ made by His death on the Cross, and contrary to express Scripture' ('Corruptions of the Church of Rome,' § 3. Works, vol. ii., p. 251. Oxford, 1846).

Bishop Beveridge.

1.

'His death was not only a true and proper sacrifice, but the only true and proper sacrifice for sin that was ever offered up in the world. For His being offered up for the sins of the whole world, there was no sin for which any other need or could be offered. . . . The Sacrament of the Lord's Supper is now ordained by Him, to set forth and commemorate the same sacrifice as now already offered up for the sins of mankind' ('Church Catechism Explained,' pp. 196, 197. London, 1704).

II.

'They all agree in the thing, avouching that in the Mass they offer up a true and perfect sacrifice to God, propitiatory for the sins of the people, even as Christ did when He offered up Himself to God as a propitiation for our sins. This, I say, is that which the Church of Rome confidently affirms, and which our Church in this Article doth as confidently deny' (Beveridge, 'On Articles,' pp. 506, 507. Oxford, 1846).

III.

'All the sacrifices of Mass are at the best but *dangerous deceits*' (*ibid.*, p. 509).

Dr. John Patrick.

'If they [the words of the canon] mean (as he that made the prayer did) that God would accept this oblation of bread and wine as He did of *Abel* and *Melchizedek* (which latter was indeed bread and wine), this had been very proper. But to make that which we offer to be Christ Himself (as they that believe in transubstantiation must expound it), and to desire God to look propitiously and benignly upon Him . . . this sense can never be agreeable to the prayer' ('Full View,' p. 171. London, 1688).

Dean Sherlock.

'It is evident to a demonstration that the Church of Rome has overthrown the death and sacrifice of Christ upon the Cross, considered as an argument of a holy life, by setting up the sacrifice of the Mass, human penances,' etc. ('Preservative Against Popery,' § 3. In Gibson's 'Preservative,' vol. xi., p. 241. London, 1848).

Answer to 'A Papist Misrepresented and Represented.'*

'The Council of Trent not only affirms *a true proper propitiatory sacrifice to be there offered up for the quick and the dead*, but denounces *anathemas* against those that deny it. So that the question is not, Whether the Eucharist may

---

* This book was published anonymously in 1686, but is acknowledged to be the work of Dr. Stillingfleet, and will be found in vol. vi. of his collected works, London, 1710.

not in the sense of antiquity be allowed to be a *commemorative sacrifice*, as it takes in the whole action; but whether in the *Mass* there be such a representation made to God of Christ's sacrifice as to be itself a true and propitiatory sacrifice for the sins of the quick and the dead?' ('Doctrines and Practices of the Church of Rome truly Represented,' p. 79. London, 1686. With the *Imprimatur* of H. Maurice, Chaplain to the Archbishop of Canterbury.)

DODWELL.

I.

'In Eucharistical sacrifices no expiation was intended to be made, but only a return of acknowledgments for favours received' ('One Altar,' p. 303. London, 1683).

II.

'Our writers, and our Church, too, do usually grant as much as I am concerned for, that it is indeed an Eucharistical sacrifice, and that this is the true sense of those passages of antiquity which are produced for this purpose. And I have shown that their principles of reasoning were against *repetition* of *propitiatory sacrifice*, which is that which is denied by our writers' (*ibid.*, pp. 311, 312).

'PAPISTS NOT MISREPRESENTED BY PROTESTANTS.'

I.

'We charge them with making the Sacrament of the Lord's Supper (as the Council of Trent defines) *a true proper propitiatory sacrifice for the quick and the dead.* And this, we say, infers an insufficiency in the sacrifice made by Christ upon the Cross' ('Reply to Reflections,' § xxii., p. 26. London, 1686. With the *Imprimatur* of C. Alston, Chaplain to the Bishop of London).

II.

'We do not charge them with *believing an insufficiency in the sacrifice made by Christ on the Cross.* Much less do we say that they are taught wholly to rely on the sacrifice of the Mass, and *to neglect the passion of Christ, and to put no hopes in His merits, and the work of our redemption.* The first is a consequence which we charge upon their doctrine and practice, but do not charge them with believing it. The second was never charged on them that I know of before. So that if there be any misrepresentation here, it must be in charging them that they believe the sacrifice of the Mass to be *a true proper propitiatory sacrifice for the quick and dead*. But this is the very definition of their council' (*ibid.*, pp. 26, 27).

Bishop John Williams, of Chichester.

'There are Articles which the two Churches do in whole or in part so differ in, that the doctrine of the Church of England cannot be the doctrine of the Church of Rome, nor the doctrine of the Church of Rome be the doctrine of the Church of England. Such are most, if not all, of the following Articles, viz. : Article VI. Of the sufficiency of the holy Scriptures for salvation. . . . Article XXXI. *Of the oblation of Christ upon the Cross.* . . . These, besides several others which our Articles do not expressly mention (but are commonly the received principles of our Church), are the irreconcilable points, and which all the wit and charity in the world can no more thoroughly reconcile than light and darkness. . . . It will be evident that there is no possibility of agreement between them [the Churches] in matters of religion, of making one Church of what are so manifestly two'* ('The Difference between the Church of England and the Church of Rome.' In Gibson's 'Preservative,' vol. xiii., p. 161. London, 1848).

Grabe.

I.

'Christ accordingly, in the first Eucharist, gave thanks to God the Father, not only for

---

* See pp. 189 and 205, where 'the Opposition' in the matter of our Article XXXI. is shown by setting side by side the words of the Article, and the teaching of the Council of Trent. This work was published in answer to a book written in the interests of the Papacy, and entitled, 'The Agreement between the Church of England and the Church of Rome,' the writer of which confined himself to 'government and worship.' He followed R. H., *i.e.*, Abraham Woodhead, who (while desiring to minimize the difference between the Churches as to 'Real Presence,'—'Rational Account,' pp. 65-68, 2nd edit., 1673) went no further in the matter of the sacrifice than to state that 'Learned Protestants, together with the whole Greek and Latin Church, grant the Eucharist to be the Christian or Evangelical sacrifice, not only in respect of the action in it of praise and thanksgiving, but also in respect of the oblation to God of the mysteries in the consecration, as a commemorative or representative of the body and blood of Christ offered on the Cross' (*ibid.*, p. 268).

creation, but chiefly for redemption, the memorial Sacrament whereof He was then instituting, and by His example and precept appointed the same to be done now also by priests' (MSS. Adversaria; quoted from Tract 81, p. 377).

II.

'The English divines teach that in the holy Eucharist the body and blood of Christ, under the species, that is, the signs, of bread and wine, are* offered to God, and become a representation of the sacrifice of Christ once made upon the Cross, whereby God may be rendered propitious'† ('Distinctions of the English Church,' etc. In Tract 81, p. 379).

III.

'Of the use of it ["First Liturgy of Edward VI.," republished], namely, to show how near the first reformers of the Church of England kept to the primitive institution of Jesus Christ, and the practice of His immediate followers, the

---

* See below, Appendix, Note B.
† See above, Introduction, p. 35, 36.

holy Apostles and the ancient Christians, although they laid aside the later Popish abuses' (Preface to 'Edward VI.'s First Liturgy.' In Tract 81, pp. 379, 380).

IV.

'Not to mention the elevation of the consecrated elements to be worshipped by priest and all people, as Jesus Christ Himself, both God and man in person, whom the Church of Rome believeth to be substantially and wholly present under the outward figures of bread and wine, nor to speak of some other faults of less moment, our reformers justly redressed that grievous and grand sacrilege' (*ibid.*, p. 381).

V.

'Our English bishops were wiser, and although they left the Church or Court of Rome upon the account of their intolerable abuses,* yet as

---

* For a clearing of some misconceptions concerning Grabe's doctrine, see Waterland, Works, vol. iv., pp. 726, 727. Waterland says, p. 727 : 'The complaint [of Deylingius] now is, not that Dr. Grabe asserted the sacrifice of the Mass (which he heartily abhorred), but that he rejected the real, local, or corporal presence, such as the Papists or Lutherans contend for : in which most certainly he judged right.'

they duly kept up their holy order and episcopal dignity, so did they likewise retain the substance of the ancient liturgy' (*ibid.*, p. 381).

Archbishop Sharp.

I.

'The Romanists have invented a new sacrifice, which Christ never instituted, which the Apostles never dreamt of, which the primitive Christians would have *abhorred*, and which we, if we will be followers of them, ought never to join in' (Works, vol. v., p. 197. Oxford, 1829).

II.

'This is the Romish doctrine concerning the sacrifice of the Mass. But how groundless, how false, how absurd—nay, how *impious*—it is, I now come . . . to show' (*ibid.*, p. 198).

Leslie.

'The Papists see *their idol of transubstantiation* broken to pieces, not from the nicety and criticism of a word, but from the nature of the thing, for a representative and commemorative sacrifice must be a different thing from, but bearing a great resemblance to, the archetypal sacrifice it represents' (quoted from Tract 81, p. 292).

John Johnson.

I.

'If any have asserted the sacrifice of the Mass, I would readily grant that no reproaches are too hard, no censures too severe, against them who were guilty of attempting to introduce so *abominable a corruption*' (Johnson's Works, A.C.L., vol. i., p. 5).

II.

'The Papists hold that in the sacrifice of the Mass the whole Christ, God and man, is offered hypostatically to the Father in the Eucharist, and is to be worshipped there by men under the species of bread and wine. This doctrine is *utterly renounced* by all Protestants, by those who assert the Eucharistic oblation, as well as by those who deny it.

'The Papists assert the substantial presence of Christ's body and blood under the species of bread and wine in the Holy Eucharist, and that the sacrifice of the Cross and altar are substantially the same; but this is peremptorily *denied* by those who declare for the oblation of the Eucharist in the Church of England.

'The Papists do maintain that the sacrifice of the Mass is available for remission of sins to the dead as well as to the living. And as this is not asserted by any of our Church, so it is *heartily detested* by the author of this treatise.

'The Papists have private Masses, in which the Priest pretends to make the oblation without distributing either the body or blood to the people—nay, without any people attending—and they have many hundred such Masses to one Communion, and all this is expressly justified by the Council of Trent (Sess. XXII., c. vi.), though it be contrary to Scripture, and the practice of the primitive Church, and to several expressions even in their own Mass-book, which suppose the people to be present. *All this is condemned* by those who defend the Eucharistical oblation here in England.

'I need not tell the learned reader that the opinions here renounced are they which render the *Mass a sacrifice so odious in the sight of God, and of all well-informed Christians*' ('Propitiatory Oblation in the Holy Eucharist,' pp. 5, 6; quoted from Tract 81, pp. 310, 311).

III.

'I never elevated the elements after consecration—nay, I believe it horrible superstition in those that do it, if any such there be—and I do further solemnly declare it to be my sentiment, that to elevate and adore the Sacrament, according to the practice of the Church of Rome, is downright idolatry'* (Works, A.C.L., vol. ii., p. 25).

N. SPINCKES.

I.

'It is acknowledged on all hands that this Sacrament is a commemoration of our Saviour's

---

* For explanation of Johnson's view of 'propitiation and expiation,' see Works, A.C.L., vol. i., p. 384, and for censure of the 'unwarrantable excesses' of his system, see Waterland's Works, vol. v., pp. 150-181. See also vol. i., p. 167.

offering Himself upon the Cross . . . and so has been figuratively called a sacrifice, a commemorative . . . and Eucharistical sacrifice . . . But this will not suffice, for the Council of Trent anathematizes such as proceed no further. . . . If truly and properly *a propitiatory sacrifice*, as the Council, Catechism, and Creed teach, how will he be able to reconcile this with the Apostle's doctrine—*Where remission of sins is, there is no more offering for them.*' If no more offering, then not a new, daily, proper and propitiatory sacrifice, such as their Church teaches this to be . . . such a sacrifice as the Scripture knows nothing of, nor any one of the ancient fathers ever described it to be' ('Essay towards Proposal for Catholic Communion answered Chapter by Chapter,' pp. 142, 143. London, 1705).

II.

'The Church of Rome requiring more is guilty of the schism that comes by refusing it' (*ibid.*, p. 145).

Hickes.

I.

'The Bishop of Sarum on Article XXXI. writes of the holy Eucharist . . . "Upon these accounts we do not deny but that the Eucharist may be called a sacrifice. But still it is a commemorative sacrifice, and not propitiatory. . . ." The bishop means not propitiatory in itself, or by its own virtue, *as the Papists assert their sacrifice of the Mass to be*' (Quoted from Tract 81, p. 275).

II.

'The right understanding of the commemorative and representative sacrifice in the Eucharist is so far from reducing us to the *sacrifice of the Mass* that it secures us as a bulwark against it. . . . There is a very plain and intelligible difference between the Eucharist's being the sacrifice of the real body and blood of Christ, and its being a real sacrifice of His mystical body and blood. . . . Mystical and real differ as much as the substance and the shadow, the verity and its type, or a thing of any sort or kind from the thing that is its image. All this is comprehended in the distinction between "mystical" and "real," the one as I have said is a contradiction and bar to the other, and therefore great must be their ignorance or prejudice who cannot distinguish the pure primitive from *the Popish doctrine of the Eucharist*' (*ibid.*, pp. 283, 284).

III.

'I am confident were he [Baxter] now alive he would not so severely and unjustly censure us as the doctor doth, nor would suggest as if we wrote with an evil intention to introduce the Popish sacrifice of the Mass, as some others lately have done, against all reason and charity: first, because, as Dr. Hakewell truly observes, "the commemoration or representation of a thing must be both in nature and propriety of speech distinct from the thing it commemorates or represents;" and, secondly, because most of the writers for the Eucharistical sacrifice have also been most eminent writers against the Church of Rome in defence of the Church of England' (Treatises, A.C.L., vol. i., p. 26).

Brett.

I.

'Those who charge the doctrine of the Eucharistical sacrifice as savouring of Popery either know not what Popery is, or have no right notion of the Eucharist itself, for nothing can be more directly opposite to the doctrine of transubstantiation, or to "the sacrifices of Masses, in the which it was commonly said that the priests did offer Christ for the quick and the dead," than this doctrine of the representative sacrifice of the Eucharist' (Tract 81, p. 386).*

II.

'When we show our people the true nature of this sacrifice, that it is not the individual sacrifice of Christ Himself (for that was offered "once for all"), but only the memorial or representation of that sacrifice, they will see

---

* It is not a little remarkable that a non-juror of such extreme views as Dr. Brett (see papers on 'Eucharistic Presence,' p. 458), should have spoken of the rubrics of the Roman missal as 'corrupt, dangerous, superstitious, abominably idolatrous, theatrical, and utterly unworthy the gravity of so sacred an institution' (see Hutton's 'Anglican Ministry,' p. 60).

clearly that the *Popish sacrifice of the Mass*, wherein they pretend to offer Christ " for the quick and the dead," has no foundation in the Scripture or the ancient fathers, but is clearly opposite to them; forasmuch as the picture cannot be the man whose picture it is, nor the representative the person he represents' (*ibid.*, p. 387).

WAKE.

1.

'A third consequence of the corporeal presence of Christ in the holy Eucharist is the *sacrifice of the Mass*, in which we ought to proceed with all the caution such a point requires, as both makes up the chiefest part of the Popish worship, and is justly esteemed one of the *greatest and most dangerous errors* that offend us.

'Monsieur de Meux has represented it to us with so much tenderness, that except, perhaps, it be his foundation of the corporeal presence on which he builds, and his consequence that this service is a *true and real propitiatory sacrifice*, which his manner of expounding it we are persuaded *will never bear*, there is little in it besides but what we could readily assent to' ('Doctrine of the Church of England,' Article XXI. In Gibson's 'Preservative,' vol. xii., p. 125. London, 1848).

II.

'Let us conjure our brethren of the Church of Rome seriously to consider these things, and into what desperate consequences this great error of the corporeal presence has insensibly led them. . . . For our parts we must profess that these things give us not only a scandal, but a horror for their religion. Monsieur de Meux had certainly reason to say that this is the chiefest and most important of all our controversies, and wherein we are at farthest distance from one another' (*ibid.*, Article XXIII., pp. 130, 131).

III.

'Let the Church of Rome . . . raise their anathemas out of their councils, and banish their Masses and adorations out of their churches. . . . Till then in vain does Monsieur de Meux exhort us to consider the ways of Providence to bring us to a union, which God knows we could be glad to have on any terms but the loss of truth' (*ibid.*, p. 132).

IV.

'That it is necessary to the evangelical priesthood that they should have power to offer up Christ truly and properly as the Council of Trent defines. This we deny, and shall have reason to do so till it can be proved to us that their Mass is indeed such a sacrifice as they pretend, and that our Saviour left it as an essential part of their priesthood to offer it. For the rest, if with the Council of Trent he indeed believes the Mass to be a true and proper sacrifice, he ought not to blame us for taking it in that sense in which they themselves understand it, for certainly it is impossible for words to represent a sacrifice more strictly and properly than the Council of Trent has defined this' ('Defence of Exposition,' Article XIX. In Gibson's 'Preservative,' vol. xii., p. 212).

V.

'If I affirmed the sacrifice of the Mass to be one of those errors that most offends us, I said no more than what the Church of England has always thought of it' ('Defence of Exposition.' p. 67. London, 1686).

VI.

'To talk of an expiatory sacrifice for sin without suffering is not only contrary to Scripture, but is in the nature of the thing itself absurd. . . . The Apostle . . . concludes that Christ could not be more than *once offered*, because He could but once suffer. But to suppose that Christ in His present glorified state can suffer is such a contradiction to all the principles of our religion that the Papists themselves are ashamed to assert it. . . . We do not deny but that in a large sense this sacrament may be called a sacrifice, as the bread and wine may be called the body and blood of Christ. But that this sacrament should be a *true* and proper sacrifice, as they define the sacrifice of the Mass to be, it is altogether *false* and *impious* to assert' ('Principles of Christian Religion,' pp. 157, 158. London, 1731).

LAWRENCE (NON-JURING BISHOP).

'And 'tis only for this reason that the Article condemns the *sacrifices of Masses* for "blas-

phemous fables and dangerous deceits," because the Romanists pretended that Christ is again really offered to God in those sacrifices, that His very body and blood are substantially (and not representatively) then present at their altars, and offered to God daily by the priests for the sins of the world, making thereby these their pretended sacrifices of Christ's real body and blood equal in worth and value to His own oblation of Himself, which He offered but once upon the altar of the Cross. This is *blasphemy* with a witness, but what has all this to do with the doctrine of that sacrifice, of real bread and wine, which has been lately revived, and convincingly taught and proved by the excellent writers of our Church?' ('The Bishop of Oxford's Charge Considered,' quoted from Tract 81, p. 409).

BINGHAM.

I.

'Which [Christian priesthood] is not, as some imagine, a power to offer Christ's body and blood really upon the altar as a propitiatory sacrifice for the quick and dead (which is such a notion of the Christian priesthood as no ancient author or ritual ever mentions), but it consists in a power and authority to minister publicly according to God's appointment in holy things' (Ant., Book II., c. xix., § xv., vol. i., p. 269. London, 1843).

II.

'That we call "solitary Mass," where the priest receives alone without any other communicants, and sometimes says the office alone without any assistance; such are all those private and solitary Masses in the Roman Church, which are said at their private altars in the corners of their Churches without the presence of any but the priest alone, and all those public Masses where none but the priest receives, though there be many spectators of the action. As there is no agreement of either of these with the institution of Christ, but a direct opposition to it . . . so there is not the least footstep of any such practice in the primitive Church' (Ant., Book XV., c. iv., § iv., vol. v., pp. 159, 160).

Bishop Hooper, of Bath and Wells.

I.

'This article [of infallibility] so fundamental must have some very extraordinary support itself, not only sufficient to bear its own weight, but all that vast additional load that rests upon it. As, for example, whether these are articles of faith, and necessary to salvation : . . . "That in the Mass there is a true and proper sacrifice offered." "That it is a propitiatory sacrifice, and to be offered not only for the living, but for the dead, in purgatory." "That the priest may and does well to communicate (as they call it) alone. . . ." these are so many single propositions highly questionable, and much easier to be asserted by the Church of Rome than proved' (Works, vol. i., pp. 99, 100. Oxford, 1855).

II.

'It sufficiently appears, I presume, that the sacrament of the Body and Blood of our Lord was understood by the ancient Christians to be in the nature of an Eucharistical (not of a propitiatory) sacrifice with the Jews. But further, that this kind of sacrifice only should remain, when all the rest should cease; this also is consonant to the tradition of the Jews, as Kimchi tells us. For upon this saying of the prophet [Jeremiah xxxiii. 11] ... he comments on the last words in this manner: "The prophet says not that they shall bring sin offerings, or trespass offerings, because in that day there would be no wicked nor sinners among them, for (as he before told them) *they should all know the Lord.* And so have our masters of blessed memory told us, that in the time to come all sacrifices should cease, except the sacrifice of thanksgiving." This saying of the masters of Israel is a great truth, and better understood by Christians *who know the Lord*, and themselves so well, as to know that *the sacrifices for sin* are not ceased by the ceasing of sin, but superseded by the sacrifice made for them by their Lord and High Priest, and that *the sacrifice of thanksgiving* they are thenceforth to make is the commemoration their Lord has instituted for that their most gracious redemption' (Works, vol. i., pp. 456, 457. Oxford, 1855).

Dr. William Nicholls.

I.

'As for the name Lord's Supper (which name the Papists cannot endure to have this sacrament called by, because it destroys their notion of a propitiatory sacrifice for the living and the dead, and their use of private Mass), we find this name given to it, as the proper one belonging to it in the Apostle's time, by St. Paul himself' ('Commentary on Common Prayer: Order of Administration of Lord's Supper,' p. 1. London, 1712).

II.

'Nostri, uti vocamus, Articuli, sive Fidei Confessio . . . extra omnem dubitationem evincunt tantum Nostram Religionem a Pontificiâ, quantum Cœlum a Terrâ distare' ('Defensio Ecclesiæ Anglicanæ,' Pars I., p. 135. London, 1707).

Welchman.

I.

'Since the offering of Christ, which was once made upon the Cross, is sufficient, there is no occasion for any other; and since it is perfect, it ought not to be repeated. . . . See also St. Cyprian: "We make mention of His passion in all our sacrifices, for the passion of our Lord is the sacrifice which we offer." Where note, that though the passion of our Lord be a sacrifice, yet there cannot be a true sacrifice in the Mass unless our Lord truly suffered in the Mass, which to affirm is very shocking and absurd. . . . But if He is only offered mystically— that is, if in the Mass that one only Sacrifice, which was offered upon the Cross, is again represented upon the altar, then there is not in the Mass a true, proper, and propitiatory sacrifice as the Romanists believe, but only a commemoration of a true, proper, and propitiatory sacrifice, as the Reformed believe' ('Notes on the Articles,' pp. 95, 96. English translation, S.P.C.K.).

II.

'By what bands can these men be bound, such double dealers, and of so slippery a faith, that, according to them, one might subscribe the creed of Pius IV. or the Koran of Mahomet? . . . The man who with a different sense subscribes is guilty of a solemn falsehood; acts the part not of an honest Christian, but of a dishonest Jesuit' (*ibid.*, Preface, p. ix.).

Waterland.

I.

'That the sacrament of the Eucharist, in whole or in part, in a sense proper or improper, is a sacrifice of the Christian Church, is a point agreed upon among all knowing and sober divines, Popish, Lutheran, or Reformed. But the Romanists have so often and so grievously abused the once innocent names of oblation, sacrifice, propitiation, etc., perverting them to an ill-sense, and grafting false doctrine and false worship upon them, that the Protestants have been justly jealous of admitting those names, or scrupulously wary and reserved in the use of them' ('Review of the Doctrine of the Eucharist,' c. xii., Works, vol. iv., p. 725. Oxford, 1843).

II.

The Romanists, wanting arguments to support their *Mass sacrifice*, thought of this pretence, among others—that either their Mass must be the sacrifice of the Church, or the Church had really none; and so if the Protestants resolved to throw off the Mass, they would be left without a sacrifice, without an altar, without a priesthood, and be no longer a Church. . . . I shall pass over Bellarmine's trifling exceptions to the Protestant sacrifice (meaning the *grand sacrifice* considered in the passive sense). It is self-evident, that while we have Christ we want neither *sacrifice*, *altar*, nor *priest*, for in Him we have all; and if He is the *head* and we the body, there is the Church' ('Christian Sacrifice Explained,' Works, vol. v., pp. 125, 126. Oxford, 1843).

III.

'Even lay Christians, considered as *offering* spiritual sacrifices, are so far *priests*, according to the doctrine of the New Testament, confirmed by Catholic antiquity. But waving that nicety (as some may call it), yet certainly when spiritual sacrifices are offered up by *priests*, divinely commissioned, and in the face of a Christian congregation, they are then as proper sacrifices as any other are or can be' (*ibid.*, p. 128).

IV.

'It is of some moment that the current opinion before the Council of Trent was against the *first*

Eucharist's being an *expiatory* sacrifice, and that the Divines of Trent were almost equally divided upon that question, and that it was chiefly fear of the consequences, obvious to Protestants, which obliged the Council to controvert the then current persuasion. It is not without its weight that Jansenius, Bishop of Ghent, who died fourteen years after, was content to take in spiritual sacrifice, in order to make out some sacrifice in the first Eucharist, as to which he judged very right, for undoubtedly our Lord so sacrificed in the Eucharist, and we do it now. But no proof has been given, nor ever can be given, of our Lord's *sacrificing the elements*. He might—yea, He did—*offer* the elements for consecration (which is very different from sacrificing, being done also in baptism), or He might present them as signs and figures of a *real* sacrifice, being also signs and figures of *real* body and blood; but as they were not the *real* body and blood which they represented, so neither were they the real sacrifice, neither can it be made appear that they were any sacrifice at all' (Appendix to 'Christian Sacrifice,' Works, vol. v., p. 163).

V.

'From the third century and downwards *altar of the Cross* has been the current language, one certain argument among many, that the *sacrifice* was supposed to be made *upon the Cross*' (Works, vol. v., p. 175).

VI.

'Scripture speaks often of Christ's offering *Himself*, but never once of His offering in sacrifice the *symbols*' (Works, vol. v., p. 180).

VII.

'Our Lord, according to the accounts of the New Testament, sacrificed Himself but *once*, therefore either He did it not *in the Eucharist*, or not *upon the Cross*' (Works, vol. v., p. 180).

Ford.

'Si Christus ipse in Missa vere offertur in remissionem, vere occiditur, et sanguis Ejus vere effunditur; nam sine Sanguinis effusione nulla est remissio. Hoc certè si quid aliud, *blasphemum* est *figmentum*. Si mysticè tantum offertur, h.e. si in Missâ sacrificium illud unicum in cruce oblatum, denuo in altare repræsentetur in Missâ, non est verum, proprium, et propitiatorium, sacrificium, ut credunt Romanenses; sed tantum veri, proprii, et propitiatorii sacrificii commemoratio, uti credunt Reformati'* ('Christian Religion,' p. 308. London, 1720).

Veneer.

'That this sacrament is a true and proper sacrifice, as those of the Church of Rome define the Mass to be, is altogether *false* and *blasphemous*, because it ascribes that to the priest which the Scriptures have ascribed to Christ alone' ('Exposition of Articles,' vol. ii., p. 676. London, 1730).

Archbishop Potter.

1.

'In the Christian Church there is only one proper sacrifice which our Lord offered upon the Cross, and consequently cannot partake of any sacrifice in a literal and strict sense without allowing transubstantiation' ('Discourse of Church Government,' quoted from Tract 81, p. 403).

* Compare Welchman as quoted, p. 214.

II.

'It is not to be wondered that those of the Reformed religion have either wholly abstained from the names of sacrifice and oblation, or mentioned them with caution and reserve, in explaining this sacrament, which were used by the primitive fathers in a very true and pious sense, since they have been so grossly abused by the Papists in their doctrine of transubstantiation, which is the daily occasion of many superstitious and idolatrous practices, and has for several ages given infinite scandal both to Jews and Gentiles, and to the Church of God' (*ibid.*, p. 405).

LAW.

'The reason why this Sacrament is said in one respect to be a* "propitiatory" or "commemorative" sacrifice is only this—because you there† offer, present, and plead before God such things as are by Christ Himself said to be His "body" and "blood given for you"; but if that which is thus offered, presented, and pleaded before God is offered and pleaded before Him only for this reason, because it signifies and represents, both to God and angels and men, the great Sacrifice for all

* See Introduction, p. 35.   † See Appendix, Note B.

the world, is there not sufficient reason to consider this service as truly a sacrifice?' ('Demonstration of the Gross and Fundamental Errors of a Late Book,' quoted from Tract 81, p. 412).

Archbishop Secker.

'Indeed, every act, both of worship and obedience, is in some sense a sacrifice to God, humbly offered up to Him for his acceptance. And this sacrament in particular, being a memorial and representation of the sacrifice of Christ solemnly and religiously made, may well enough be called, in a figurative way of speaking, by the same name with what it commemorates and represents. But that He should be really and literally offered up in it is the directest contradiction that can be, not only to common sense, but also to Scripture. . . . This ordinance then was appointed, not to repeat, but to commemorate, the sacrifice of Christ' ('Lectures on Catechism,' vol. ii., p. 240. London, 1769).

Bishop Warburton.

'As it [the Last Supper] was contrived to declare the real nature of Christ's death, so it likewise served this further purpose, a purpose of great importance, to declare the ABOLITION OF SACRIFICES IN REVEALED RELIGION. For if in the most solemn act of worship, where a sacrifice always took place, a *commemoration only of a sacrifice* is celebrated, it is plain all sacrificial rites are excluded from that religion, and (if that religion be the completion of God's religious dispensations) consequently *abolished*' ('Discourse on the Lord's Supper, Works, vol. x., pp. 349, 350. London, 1811).

PROFESSOR HEY.

'As to all the sacrifices of the Mass and the sacrifice of Christ making but *one*, that seems quite a *gratis dictum* and no *argument*. Hebrews v. 3, compared with vii. 24-28, shows that no man can be a priest in the room of Christ to offer up the Christian sacrifice. Read 1 Peter iii. 18: Whatsoever completes types makes a conclusion, that therefore did Christ. On 1 Peter i. 20 we observe, that as Christ was the Lamb slain from the foundation of the world, He must be the only propitiatory Sacrifice for the sins of *all mankind*. According to Hebrews x. 2, 3, whatever sacrifice is *repeated* cannot take away sin. Either Christ *suffers* in the sacrifice of the Mass, or he does not; if He suffers He must be ever suffering (against Phil. ii. 9; Heb. ix. 26), if not it is no real sacrifice; add Heb. ix. 22: I will not detain you with producing more authorities in so plain a case. *Private* Masses are against 1 Cor. x. 17; xii. 13, etc.

'Masses may be called *blasphemous* as degrading Christ, dragging Him, as it were, down from heaven for a few *sous*—merely to describe the thing seems a sort of blasphemy, a poor priest *labouring* with a *wafer* in the *occupation* and craft of offering up our blessed Lord! treating a happy and glorious Being "crowned with glory and honour" (Heb. ii. 9) as wretched and despicable—nay, *numberless* priests doing this at the same time, and muttering at numberless altars. Books of travels which relate these facts must be shocking to every serious reader' ('Lectures in Divinity,' vol. ii., pp. 580, 581. Cambridge, 1841).

BISHOP TOMLINE.

'The principle upon which the Popish Masses are founded is not authorized by Scripture. . . . The sacrifices of Masses may therefore justly be called "*fables*," since they have no authority in Scripture; and they are "*blasphemous*," inasmuch as they derogate from the sufficiency of the death and passion of Christ as an expiation for the sins of mankind' ('Exposition of XXXIX. Articles,' pp. 483, 484. London, 1835).

Bishop Cleaver.

'" Every priest," says this Apostle, "appeareth daily ministering, and ofttimes offereth one manner of offering, which can never take away sins. But this man, after He had offered one Sacrifice for sins, sitteth for ever at the right hand of God" . . . The sacrifices of the Mosaic law were therefore to be repeated so often as the acts or omissions producing legal uncleanness render them needful. But a full remission of the sins of mankind being promised as the privilege of the covenant purchased by the sacrifice of Christ's death, for it is said "their sins and iniquities will I remember no more," there remaineth, to use the Apostle's words, "no more offering for sins." To attribute therefore *atonement or expiation to any subsequent rite is to contradict the whole sense of Scripture*"' ('Sermon before University of Oxford, Nov. 28, 1790.' Oxford, 1791).

APPENDIX.

NOTE A. (See p. 84.)

On the Publication of Ælfric's Homily by Archbishop Parker.

Strype tells us, in his life of Archbishop Parker: 'Among the ancient books and treatises which our prelate, greatly studious of antiquity, occasionally set forth, I make little doubt to add that Saxon sermon (which as near as I can guess about this year [1566] appeared abroad) of the Paschal Lamb, and of the Sacramental body and blood of Christ, written in the old Saxon tongue before the Conquest, and appointed in the reign of the Saxons to be pronounced to the people before they should receive the Communion on Easter Day, which sermon speaks of that Sacrament plainly and evidently contrary to the novel doctrine of the Papal transubstantiation. The book is intituled, *A testimony of antiquity, shewing the ancient faith of the Church of England, touching the Sacrament of the body and blood of the Lord here publicly preached, and also received, in the Saxon time, above* 700 *years ago.*'

No doubt the special point for which this 'Testimony' was published was its witness to the *significant* sense in which the words of institution had then been understood. 'The Apostle Paul sayth, that the Israelites did eat the same ghostly meat, and drink the same ghostly drink: because the heavenly meate that fedde them fourtye yeares, and the water which from the stone did flowe, had signification of Christ's bodye, and his bloude, that now be offered daylye in God's Churche. It was the same which we now offer: not bodely, but ghostly' (Thomson's edition, p. 31).

This was an echo of that teaching of St. Augustin, of which Rupert of Deutz had declared that if an angel from heaven should proclaim it, it must not be received (see 'Lectures on Lord's Supper,' p. 64). And it was clearly as contradictory to the Romish doctrine of the Real Presence as it was to the augmentation conception of Rupert.

Yet the fact of this homily being published by the authority of the Bishops was afterwards appealed to by an anonymous (and somewhat scurrilous) writer as evidence 'For the Mass's being a sacrifice for the living and the dead.' 'So Abbot Ælfrike . . . an author, the rather to be esteemed, as having had no less than the two Archbishops, and thirteen of Queen Elizabeth's Bishops at once for his vouchers upon his first publication' (extract of the 'First Liturgy of King Edward VI. . . . showing how far it was Popishly affected,' p. 22).

And this writer's example has recently been followed, unwittingly and unwillingly (we may be sure), by two able and learned Presbyters of the Church of England.

No doubt, by a singular inadvertence, the authors of 'De Hierarchia Anglicanâ' have alleged this edition of Ælfric's homily as witnessing to the views of the English Reformed Church on the doctrine of the Mass.

Thus they have written: 'Matthæus enim Parker, jam Archiepiscopus Cantuariensis, cum homiliam ab antecessore suo Ælfrico conscriptam typis mandavissit, plane docuit, "Ipsum quidem Christum semel passum, nec minus passionem Ejus in Missa per mysterium S. Eucharistiæ quotidie renovatam esse." Neque id merum erat antiquitatis testimonium, quindecim enim Episcopi hujus libelli doctrinam subscriptis nominibus confirmarunt. Multi, fatemur, contra dixerunt; non illi quidem veri Ecclesiæ Anglicanæ defensores, sed potius lues Calviniana, qui in Ecclesiâ demorabantur, beneficia corripiebant, dignitates sibi arrogabant.'

The words of Ælfric's homily are these: 'Once suffered Christ by Himself, but yet, nevertheless, His suffering is daily renewed at the Mass through mystery of the holy housel. Therefore the holy Mass is profitable both to the living and to the dead' (p. 36, Thomson's edition, 1849).

If the prefatory certificate had not unhappily escaped the notice of the authors of ' De Hierarchia Anglicanâ,' they would surely have seen that the Archbishops and Bishops who signed it (so far as they are responsible for the publication) must no longer take a place among those whom they regard as the 'veri Ecclesiæ Anglicanæ defensores,' but must be classed among those whom they designate as 'lues Calviniana,' seeing that this doctrine of Ælfric's lies at the root of the very first point to which the Archbishops and Bishops take exception as 'not consonant to sound doctrine.' The homily is not allowed to go forth without a disclaimer of the doctrine of a Mass-sacrifice profitable to the quick and dead (cf. p. 81 above).

On the subject of this homily and its publication by Parker, see Strype's 'Life of Parker,' book iii., c. xv., pp. 237 *sqq*. See also Soames' 'Bampton Lectures,' pp. 384-389 and 421 *sqq*. Also papers on 'Eucharistic Presence,' p. 652.

If it were possible to restrict the subscriptions of the other Bishops to the mere certification (see Perry's 'Declaration on Kneeling,' p. 218), Parker's name would remain responsible for the doctrinal statement.

Much of the homily, as Archbishop Ussher has shown, was taken from the Book of Ratramn, and (as Dr. Moule truly states) 'the passages which corresponded were just those which were supposed by the Romanists in the sixteenth century to be the forgery of the Reformers' (Ridley's 'Brief Declaration,' p. 210).

The doctrinal statement is in full accord with what we know of Parker's doctrinal views. See 'Papers on Eucharistic Presence,' pp. 633-653. See also Parker's ' De Antiquitate Britannicæ Ecclesiæ,' pp. 508, 512. London, 1729. It is a strange mistake, indeed, by which Parker has been represented as one of very different views. He was regarded by Reformers of his own day as a man ' teres atque rotundus et sinceræ religionis assertor vehemens' (see Cox, in 'Zurich Letters,' i., p. 187).

Fuller wrote : ' He [Parker] confuted the character which one gives of antiquaries, "that generally they are either superstitious or supercilious," his skill in antiquity being attended with soundness of doctrine and humility of manners' (Fuller's 'History,' vol. ii., p. 285. Edition Oxford, 1845).

NOTE B. (See p. 123 ; see also pp. 21, 96, 97, 195.)

ON THE TWO DISTINCT SENSES OF THE VERB ' TO OFFER.'

It will be noted that Bishop Bedell acknowledges ' we do offer sacrifice for the quick and dead,' the statement being immediately guarded against misinterpretation by qualifying explanation.

So the Cologne Council of 1536, under Archbishop Hermann, had said : ' Immolamus hostiam pro vivis et defunctis, dum pro illis Patrem per Filii mortem deprecamur ' (cap. xxvii., fol. xxix *a*. Col., 1538).

And so Jewel: 'Thus we offer up Christ, that is to say, an example,* a commemoration, a remembrance of the death of Christ. This kind of sacrifice was never denied, but M. Harding's real sacrifice was yet never proved' (Works, P.S., ii., p. 729).

So also Brevint: 'We must also celebrate, and *in a manner offer to God*, and expose and lay before Him the holy memorials of that great Sacrifice on the Cross. . . . But that we should offer also Christ Himself, our Lord and our God, to whom we must offer ourselves; it is a piece of devotion never heard of among men, till the Mass came in to bring such news' ('Depth and Mystery,' p. 30).

So, too, Bishop Buckeridge: 'Though these be not *idem sacrificium* . . . yet it is *idem sacrificatum* . . . Christ crucified, that is, represented to God, and communicated to us. . . . In Baptism, in like manner . . . we do as it were, *offer up Christ crucified* by way of representation' (quoted in Tract 81, p. 86).

And so Archbishop Wake (in even stronger language): 'Whilst thus with faith we represent to God the death of His Son for the pardon of our sins, we are persuaded that we incline His mercy the more readily to forgive them. We do not, therefore, doubt but that this presenting to God Almighty this sacrifice of our blessed Lord is a most effectual manner of applying His merits to us' ('Exposition of the Doctrine of the Church of England,' p. 63. London, 1687).

But the language of Bishop Bedell should be specially compared with the words of Ridley (spoken in reply to the statement that 'a council says that the priest doth offer an unbloody sacrifice of the body of Christ'). 'I say it is well said, if it be rightly understood. . . . It is called unbloody, and is offered after a certain manner and in a mystery, and

---

* Referring to quotation just made from Chrysostom, 'Hoc sacrificium examplar illius est.'

as a representation of that bloody sacrifice, and he doth not lie who saith Christ to be offered' (see Moule's edition of 'Brief Declaration,' p. 289). It is important to mark clearly the distinction between two senses of the verb *to offer* as employed by divines in this relation. (1) In the one sense it is used to signify '*the offering symbolically to view*,' and is, therefore, nearly equivalent to *pleading*—pleading in the sacramental remembering, and showing forth the Lord's death. It indicates the mystical and representative pleading of the One Sacrifice once for all sacrificially offered and accepted for the remission of sins (see Goode, 'Divine Rule,' vol. ii., pp. 364, 365, 382, 398, 404). In this sense (however in prevalent use among the Fathers, after the time of Cyprian) it is not found in holy Scripture (nor in the Book of Common Prayer), but (with explanation and caution that it should be 'rightly understood') it has been frequently allowed and accepted by English divines as consonant with Protestant doctrine (see Waterland, Works, vol. v., p. 286, and especially pp. 129 and 183 ; and vol. i., p. 206).

In this sense it was admitted by the Puritan Perkins, who wrote : 'In this sense the faithful, in their prayers, do offer Christ as a sacrifice unto God the Father for their sins, in being wholly carried away in their minds and affections unto that only and true Sacrifice, thereby to procure and obtain God's greater favour unto them' ('Demonstration of the Problem ; Sacrifice of the Mass,' Works, vol. ii., p. 551. London, 1617).

In this sense it was accepted and used even by Baxter, who wrote: 'He hath ordained . . . that by faith and prayer they might, as it were, offer Him up to God—that is, might show the Father that sacrifice, once made for sin, in which they trust' ('Christian Directory,' Part II., c. xxiv., § 2 ; Works, vol. iv., p. 316. London, 1830). And in some such unsacrificial sense Bossuet would apparently desire to explain Christ's *offering* Himself up in the Eucharist, 'according to the expression of the holy Fathers of the Church' ('Exposition of the Doctrine of the Catholic Church,' p. 146; see also pp. 141, 135. Paris, 1672). But this is certainly not 'according to the expression' of the Council of Trent, nor of his own language (in its natural acceptation) as found in p. 137. It is, in fact, just explaining away what he there calls 'a most true and real sacrifice.'

Bossuet's book was never approved by the doctors of the Sorbonne, and was condemned as scandalous and pernicious by the University of Louvain (see 'Romish Mass and English Church,' p. 26).

(2) In the other sense it is used to signify the real sacrificial oblation of the *hostia* to God the Father on the visible altar by the action (in some sort) of the priest then and there. And this it is which (notwithstanding all minimizing explanations of its *relation* to the sacrifice of the Cross in the past) our Divines have so constantly and consistently regarded as the blasphemy of the Mass (see especially Calixtus, as quoted in Cosin's Works, vol. v., pp. 350, 351, A.C.L.).

It is important also to observe that the first sense naturally *implies* the Real Absence, and the second sense *requires* the Real Presence (in the Romish sense) *sub speciebus*. It is of the very essence of the Mass that in it is the *hypostatical* oblation of the Body and Blood of Christ. This is strongly insisted upon even by Bossuet (pp. 140, 149). It needed no special insight into the Romish doctrine to see clearly (with Bishop Andrewes) that with transubstantiation taken away the sacrifice of the Mass must fall to pieces. Nothing but commemoration remains when the Corporal Presence is gone.

It was what Romish divines constantly insisted on, that

their teaching of the sacrifice was held together by, and was built upon, the doctrine of the Corporal Presence. Indeed, in Bellarmine's teaching the Presence is for the very purpose of the sacrifice. He says: 'Eucharistia potuisset vere et proprie sacramentum esse, etiamsi Christi Corpus reipsa non contineret. Quæ igitur causa est cur debuerit necessario Eucharistia Christi Corpus reipsa continere, nisi ut posset vere, et proprie Deo Patri a nobis offerri, et proinde sacrificium esse vere ac proprie dictum?' ('De Missa,' Lib. I., cap. xxii., c. 1021; see 'Romish Mass and English Church,' p. 89; and 'Eucharistic Worship,' pp. 177, 178).

But it may be asked—Do all Roman Catholic divines accept the teaching of Bellarmine? and do not some beside Bossuet speak of the *offering* in the first sense? And it may be answered, that undoubtedly some do so use the word *offer* in the sense of *offering to view* the One Sacrifice perfected in the past, *i.e.*, and apparently in the sense which should naturally imply the Real Absence, and this in connection with the minimized sense of propitiation (see 'Dangerous Deceits,' p. 72); but that they all (as their position demands), with very few exceptions, have something to set in front of this—something which faith is to look to in the very offering (in the other sense) of the priest on the altar— something which (however dependent) is really distinct from the sacrifice of Christ on the Cross, and which requires and depends upon the Real Presence of Christ's body and blood *sub speciebus* (see Dean Field as quoted above, pp. 96, 97; and Cosin as quoted, pp. 165, 166).

This strange inconsistency may be very well illustrated by a reference to the teaching of the Presbyter Cardinal Franzelin.

It is impossible to conceive or desire anything more satisfactory than Franzelin's teaching of the one atonement by the one perfect sacrifice, oblation and satisfaction, made by Christ on the Cross (see his 'De S. S. Eucharistiâ,' Part II.; Theses v. vi. vii., pp. 326-335). It is impossible to read it without thankfulness for his faithful testimony to this truth. Indeed, *so far* it might well be desired that all Protestant theologians had given by their trumpets as certain a sound.

And consistently with this we find him speaking of the Eucharistic *offering* as the offering in representation and exhibition of the perfect sacrifice *once offered*. Thus he writes: 'Sistet et offert se Christus in hoc incruento sacrificio ut victimam, formaliter quatenus meritum nostræ redemptionis et satisfactionem pro nostris peccatis complevit in sacrificio cruento, et sub formali ratione hujus meriti et satisfactionis completæ hic jugiter se offert, ac proinde totum illud meritum consummatum continuo renovata oblatione Deo Patri repræsentat et exhibet' (p. 371).

Again: 'Satisfactio intelligitur objective ipsum opus quo satisfit pro injuriâ illatâ, impetratio autem et interpellatio potest dici etiam meriti olim consummati repræsentatio, ut vi illius beneficia concedantur' (p. 372). And again he speaks of the 'sacrificium, quo satisfactio in cruce consummata pro determinatis peccatoribus divino conspectui exhibetur' (p. 376).

So far Franzelin might almost seem to take his part among those followers of Vasquez who are accused by Cardinal Cienfuegos of reducing the sacrifice of the altar to a 'nuda commemoratio sacrificii in cruce peracti,' and whose view was thought to commend itself for this 'quod sit facilior et eâ admissâ Protestantes jam nihil habeant, cur in Missâ verum sacrificium offerri negent' (pp. 392, 393, see Forbes, 'Considerationes Modestæ,' vol. ii., p. 580, A.C.L.).

But he cannot allow himself to be classed with such, nor with the followers of Lessius, who only add to the commemoration the *vera separatio vi verborum*. And, therefore, while desiring to shield Vasquez from the charge of Cienfuegos and the anathema of Trent, he has his own way (following de Lugo, Ulloa, Viva, and others, pp. 402, 403) of making the Eucharist in itself a true and proper sacrifice ('verum sacrificium in se,' pp. 394, 395). It is by the 'exinanitio' in which Christ reduces Himself in the Eucharist 'quod manens in suâ plenitudine ac perfectione ad dexteram Patris, simul induerit in altaribus Ecclesiæ militantibus modum existendi sacramentalem ac statum cibi et potus' (p. 402, see p. 397). 'Talis "exinanitio" ad exprimendam majestatem absoluti dominii Dei et satisfactionem pro reatibus nostris morte completam non solum satis intelligitur ut vere et proprie sacrificalis; sed etiam, excepto sacrificio cruento in cruce, nullam sublimiorem ac profundiorem rationem veri et proprii sacrificii concipere possumus' (p. 405).

'Sicut enim Christus Redemptor sacrificatus est per oblationem corporis sui semel, et semel intravit in sancta per proprium sanguinem; ita quotidie se *offert* ministerio sacerdotum sese constituens per corpus et sanguinem suam in statu cibi et potus sub speciebus panis et vini' (p. 413).

So then from a representative offering, or presenting representatively to view the finished and perfect oblation of the Cross, we are brought back again to a *real* (not representative) offering of a *real* (not commemorative) sacrifice of Christ's body and blood, which is not the sacrifice of the Cross, though almost as sublime as that, and which is not 'one' nor 'once,' but daily multiplied and repeated (see p. 370, and especially note in p. 387). And the language of the Fathers is translated from the region of representation to that of reality—such language as this: 'In sacramento omni die populis immolatur'—'Pro nobis iterum in hoc mysterio immolatur' (p. 399). And this sacrifice has its efficacy not only 'ex opere operantis,' but also 'ex opere operato' (p. 368).

And that this sacrifice is relative deducts (in his teaching) nothing from its reality. He says: 'Esse *sacrificium relativum* duo significat, esse scilicet in se verum et proprium sacrificium . . . et insuper habere relationem ad alium sacrificium' (p. 389).

And so he expounds the words of institution of real blood in the sacred Supper as well as of the future blood-shedding on the Cross: 'Hic est Sanguis meus, qui pro multis effunditur sacrificio reali sed effusione mystica (representante); qui pro multis effundetur sacrificio et effusione reali ac per presens sacrificium representata' (pp. 386, 387).

'Divinus Redemptor in ipsâ institutione hanc distinctam positionem corporis et sanguinis sub speciebus panis et vini declarat esse "effusionem sanguinis." Dum scilicet habet præ oculis effusionem realem in cruce, et sacrificium præsens corporis et sanguinis distinctim sub speciebus panis et vini tanquam realem representationem illius, eodem nomine complectitur sacrificium repræsentans et sacrificium repræsentatum' (p. 386).

All this, I trust, may help to show how impossible it is for Roman Catholic theologians to *rest* in that sense of *offer* which alone has been approved by English divines, and which alone can be made to harmonize with the teaching of the Epistle to the Hebrews. How can such a sense satisfy the requirements of the Canons of Trent or the creed of Pope Pius?

And how can any other sense escape the just condemnation of our Article XXXI.?

The offering (in the sense allowed) is no *re-presenting* of any redemptive sacrifice (though it may be allowed to include a representation of it), but it may rather be compared (of course with an imperfect comparison) to the showing of the receipt for a ransom price already paid (see 'Recent Teachings Concerning the Eucharistic Sacrifice,' p. 24).

We may shrink from using comparisons which may seem to bring truths of Divine wisdom down to anything like the level of human and earthly transactions. But if it is important to make clear the distinction between the two senses of *offering*, I think we may safely say (with reverent caution) that the *offering of the sacrifice to view* is no more a *sacrificial offering* than the displaying of the voucher of an account paid is the same thing as the settling of the account by payment.

It is no μνημόσυνον to be placed on an altar, and requires the service of no *sacerdotium*, save the royal priesthood of thankful believers.

It was excellently said in the Privy Council Judgment in the Bennett case : 'The distinction between an act by which a satisfaction for sin is made, and a devotional rite by which the satisfaction so made is represented and pleaded before God, is clear, though it is liable to be obscured, not only in the apprehension of the ignorant, but by the tendency of theologians to exalt the importance of the rite till the distinction well-nigh disappears' (p. 299, edit. Stephens).

NOTE C. (See p. 62 ; see also pp. 124, 183, 192, 202.)

ON THE MASS-DOCTRINE OF SALMERON, AND ON THE DEPENDENT CHARACTER OF THE MASS-SACRIFICE.

If I rightly understand the language of Salmeron (about which I would not speak too confidently), there are in his view two sacrifices, viz., that of the Supper, and that of the Cross, both of infinite value, each distinct and (in some sense) independent* (see quotations in text, p. 61, and below, No. 1), yet so connected that the one is (in some sense) conducive to the other, and that in such sort that (in a manner) the *opus operatum* of the other is dependent upon it (see quotations, Nos. 6 and 10, below).

In contradistinction to these two infinite sacrifices is the sacrifice of the Mass, the value and efficacy of which is finite (see quotation, No. 8, below), and which, therefore, is to be daily renewed, repeated, and iterated (see quotations, Nos. 8, 11, and 12, below), and that as a provision for the expiation of daily post-baptismal sins (see quotation, No. 3, below). Each Mass is a distinct oblation (see quotation, No. 8, below), distinct from that of the two infinite sacrifices, and from that of every other finite Mass-sacrifice. But all the distinct Mass-sacrifices (though true and propitiatory sacrifices in themselves, see quotations, Nos. 3 and 12, below) are dependent for their efficacy on one or other, or both, of the two infinite sacrifices (see quotations, Nos. 8 and 11, below). Sometimes they are represented as dependent on the sacrifice of the Supper (see quotations, Nos. 4 and 11, below), sometimes on that of the Cross (see quotations, Nos. 2, 5, and 9, below). And this dependence is in such sort that the many distinct finite sacrifices become so included or contained in the infinite, that they lose (in some sort) their plurality (see quotation, No. 12, below) in this unifying connection (see quotation, No. 5, below). The efficacy of the finite sacrifices consists in the application of the infinite sacrifices (see quotation, No. 4, below).

---

* Inasmuch as one does not borrow sacrificial efficacy from the other, but each derives its value immediately from the Person and perfections (more conspicuously than from the redeeming *work* or merit, the view of which is not to be confined to the *Death*) of Christ. See quotations, Nos. 1 and 7.

The following quotations are here given to assist the reader in forming his own judgment on this matter. They are taken from the 'Comment. in Evangelicam Historiam,' tom. ix., edit. Coloniæ Agrippinæ, 1602-1604:

(1) 'Quanquam omnes actiones suas Christus Patri pro nobis obtulerit, et propterea dici possint oblationes; non tamen omnes sunt sacrificia, sed duæ tantum, nempe oblatio sui ipsius in cœna, et oblatio sui ipsius in cruce: quia illis duabus tantum accessit actio mystica. Quæ, ut exemplo aliquo illustrentur, sit v. g. vitis viginti palmitibus prædita producentibus uvas albas, quorum nullus accipiat virtutem productivam ab aliquo alio palmite, sed quivis a vite ipsa immediate. Ponamus deinde, duos palmites supremos uvas tam nigras, quam albas proferre. Ad hunc modum, omnes Christi actiones a persona Verbi, et charitate humanitatis Christi in infinitum promerendi vim habent, et ob id expiandi peccata, et satisfaciendi apud Deum' (Tract. 31, p. 247).

(2) 'Ut maxime demus non esse sacrificium sine mactatione, in sacrificio Missæ asserimus illam præcedere: eadem enim est hostia, et oblatio hæc atque illa quæ in cruce: cumque illa mactatio infiniti fuit valoris, non eget nova mactatione ut repetatur, quia satis est illam semel factam repræsentari. Etsi igitur hostia nostra viva sit, et incruenta in seipsa: repræsentatione tamen ac recordatione cruenta est, ac mortua' (Tract. 31, p. 242).

(3) 'Ratio enim peccati, et fiduciæ in Deo collocandæ exigebat, post Baptismum aliquod institui sacrificium. Nam ubicunque est expiatio peccati, ibi est hostia, et sacrificium, in quo omnia Sacramenta nostra valent. . . . Si igitur talem ac tantam, expiandi peccata ac scelera, rationem in hoc sacrificio incruento sitam videmus, merito ingentes Deo gratias agere debemus, qui nostræ fragilitati sublevandæ, atque confirmandæ tantum antidotum præparavit' (Tract. 31, pp. 248, 249).

(4) 'Ut oratio Christi applicatur nobis per nostras orationes, ita Christi oblatio, sive in cœna, sive in cruce, per eam quam faciunt Sacerdotes oblationem in Eucharistiâ, nobis communicantur' (Tract. 31, p. 244 b).

(5) 'Nec sunt plures oblationes: quoniam omnes illæ referuntur ad illam crucis, et in ea virtute continentur' (Tract. 31, p. 244 b).

(6) 'Non igitur derogat sacrificium Christi in cœna cruento crucis sacrificio, sicut nec fluvius irrigans terram, derogat ipsi mari, quia mare est, quod tacite mittit aquas fluvio, ut possit irrigare, et in virtute ejus irrigat: atque in hunc modum opus operatum hujus sacrificii a cruce pendet' (Tract. 31, p. 248 b).

(7) 'Quod autem cruenta hostia, id est, pessio, sive mors Christi non excludat, imo includat alias præcedentes actiones, probatur efficaciter . . . tunc autem non cœpit obedientia Christi, sed ab incarnatione, et per totam vitam usque ad mortem protensa est, et per eam meruit esse mundi Salvator' (Tract. 31, p. 247 b).

(8) 'Quod ergo certus, et finitus sit gratiæ fructus, qui ex vi sacrificii, et institutione Christi colligitur, probatur. Primo, quia minus est meritum oblationis Christi in sacrificio Missæ, quam fuerit sacrificii meritum in cruce peracti. Nam ibi oblata sunt Deo passio Filii Ejus, realis, et ignominiosa pariter, et afflictione plena mors, quam ex obedientia, et charitate sustinuit: quare meritum satisfactionis illius hostiæ suo jure debuit esse infinitum. At in Missæ sacrificio commemoratio, et repræsentatio illius passionis, et mortis, in vero tamen Christi corpore, et sanguine sub panis, et vini speciebus offertur. . . . Christus, qui summa sapientia est, et cum ratione cuncta operatur, non posuit tantum fructum in repræsentatione suæ mortis, quantum in sua hostia cruenta sibi comparavit: in cujus rei signum **passionem suam**, utpote infiniti fructus, et pro-

pitiationis, non repetivit : Hostiæ vero incruenta oblationem quotidie repeti voluit, quod finitus est, et in dies singulos colligendus. Habet præterea aliud discrimen hæc hostia ab illa cruenta, quod illam, cum viator esset, et tempore quo mereri poterat, obtulit : at in Eucharistia Christus non habet ullum novum meritum, cum beatus, et comprehensor, extraque tempus omne merendi existat. Si quis ergo fructus est meriti, aut satisfactionis in hac hostia incruenta, ad antiquum meritum in cruce comparatum referendum est ' (Tract. 33, p. 265 b).

(9) 'Nec est novum Missam offerre aut pro peccatis, aut pro satisfactionibus quæ pro peccatis debentur: cum Passio Christi sit, quæ offertur in eâ ' (Tract. 33, p. 260 b).

(10) 'Res contentæ in hoc Sacramento, sunt infiniti meriti, et satisfactionis, et in infinitum Deo per se gratæ, nempe Corpus et Sanguis Jesu Christi, qui Deus, et homo est, qui propter Crucis obedientiam meritum sibi infinitum apud Patrem comparavit, ut possit pro omnium peccatis satisfacere, eosque Patri reconciliare ' (Tract. 33, p. 264 a).

(11) 'Ista consequentia non valet, Christus obtulit in cœna cum infinito merito, ergo non est quod nos offeramus incruentam hostiam Deo; imo ob id obtulit, ut id offerre non tantum verbis, sed etiam factis doceret, et ut sua illa infiniti pretii oblatione in cœna celebrata efficaciam et virtutem tribueret omnibus nostris incruenti sacrificii oblationibus, quas in Novo Testamento propter Christi præceptum iteramus ' (Tract. 33, p. 267 a).

(12) 'Iteratur ergo hæc hostia, ut Christi præcepto pareamus, et ut remissionem novi alicujus peccati in dies admissi, quod antea expiatum non erat, impetramus . . . denique ut unum, et idem donum hoc sacrificio pluries oblato efficacius a Deo obtinere valeamus ' (Tract. 31, p. 267 b).

In maintaining the finite efficacy of the Mass, Salmeron

was, of course, agreeing with most other Romish divines of note. It seems strange that he should have failed to see that his argument against an infinite value in the Mass might (in the main) be applied also against the infinite character of the sacrifice *in cœna*.

It is believed that these quotations will at least suffice to make it evident that Salmeron was far enough from consistently attributing anything like an independent character to the efficacy of the Mass-sacrifice.

On the other hand, the fact that complaints were made to the Pope by the Queen-mother of Francis II., of France, of the teaching that the sacrifice of the Mass-priest was more available than the very sacrifice of Christ upon the Cross (see Meyer, ' Catechism Explained,' p. 519. London, 1623), may fairly be taken as evidence tending to confirm the opinion expressed in the text (p. 58) that in the darkness of extreme superstition among 'the ignorant and vulgar' there may have been a tendency to regard the Mass-sacrifice as practically independent, or, at any rate, to disregard, if not to lose sight of, its dependent character. If the possibility of such an error had been altogether out of the question, the friar would hardly have dared to preach such a doctrine, and if he had, there would have been no need for any alarm at the consequence of such teaching. ' No magnifier of the Mass ' (says Meyer) ' durst have sung so high a note but in a Church where the true remembrance of Christ's death is so obscured and falsified by the bastard Mass ' (see above, p. 120).

In the view of the sacrifice of the Mass as of more avail than that of the Cross, it is difficult to suppose that the greater efficacy was regarded as dependent on the less.

The same conclusion might, I believe, probably be drawn from the words of Gardiner, ' When men add unto the Mass an opinion of satisfaction or of a new redemption, then do they put it to another use than it was ordained for.' (Dixon, III., 264. See 'Church Quarterly Review,' April, 1896, p. 41.) Gardiner would hardly have so spoken if anything like such a notion had been an unheard-of thing. Neither would Luther have said, 'Cur jam aperte concionentur pro peccatis post Baptismum commissis Christum non satisfecisse sed tantum pro culpa originali' ('Conciones ad 16 Joan,' *ibid.*).

Other sayings of Reformers can hardly fail, I think, to leave the impression that the teaching of the monks *did* tend sometimes to produce some such notions among the ignorant. See 'Dangerous Deceits,' p. 41.

INDEX OF AUTHORITIES

QUOTED AND REFERRED TO.

Abbott, Bishop Robert, 101-103
Ælfric, 84, 225
Aliphanus, 62
Alley, Bishop, 89, 90
Andrewes, Bishop, 7, 8, 108, 109
Answer to 'Papist Misrepresented,' 190

Babington, Bishop, 103, 104
Bancroft, Archbishop, 94, 95
Barbon, 176
Barclay, 35
Barrow, Dr. Isaac, 166
Baxter, 230
Bayly, Bishop, 117, 118
Bedell, Bishop, 7, 122, 123
Bellarmine, 232
Berington, 'Memoirs of Panzani,' 28
Beveridge, Bishop, 188, 189
Bilson, Bishop, 100, 101
Bingham, 209, 210
Birkbek, 142, 143
Bossuet, 231
Bramhall, Archbishop, 26-28, 153-155
Brett, 38, 204

Brevint, 180, 181, 229
Buckeridge, Bishop, 109-111, 229
Bull, Bishop, 10, 48, 187, 188
Burnet, Bishop, 7, 12

Callixtus, 231
Canons of 1640, 132, 133
Cardwell's 'Synodalia,' 6
Carr's 'Life of Ussher,' 7
Carter, Canon T. T., 96
Casaubon, i., 35
'Christian Remembrancer,' 49, 51
Churton, 85
Cienfuegos, 233
Clagett, Dr. Wm., 12
Cleaver, Bishop, 224
Cooper, Bishop T., 82, 83
Cosin, Bishop, 162-166
Courayer, 41
Coverdale, 80, 81
Cowper, Bishop William (of Galloway), 106, 107
Crakanthorp, 112, 113
Cranmer, 75, 76
Cudworth, 173
Cyprianus Anglicus, 30, 31

Davenant, Bishop, 123, 124
Davenport (Sancta Clara), 39, 56
De Hierarchia Anglicana, 63, 226
De Lugo, 234
Dodwell, 191, 192
Dowden, Bishop, 42
D'Oyly's 'Life of Sanderson,' 8, 11

Elis, J., 155, 156
Ellis, 185
Enchiridion Theologicum Anti-Romanum, 12

Featley, 124-126
Ferne, 143
Field, Bishop, 113, 114
Field, Dean, 95-98
Forbes, Bishop (Edinburgh), 24, 116, 233
Forbes, J. (of Corse), 126, 127
Ford, 218
Franzelin, 232, 233
Fulke, 88
Fuller, 134

Gauden, Bishop, 152, 153
Geste, 74, 75
Goode, Dean, 31, 40, 50
Goode on 'Eucharist,' 13
Grabe, 195-197
Grendal, Archbishop, 86

Hacket, Bishop, 159, 160
Haddon, 79
Hall, Bishop, 136, 137
Hallam, 29
Hammond, 9, 145, 148
Hayward, J., 3
Hermann, Archbishop, 228
Hey, 222, 223
Heylyn, 31-33, 134, 149-152

Hickes, Dr. G., 36, 37, 202, 203
Hook, Dean, 31
Hooker, 4, 92-94
Hooper, Bishop, 78, 79
Hooper, Bishop George, 12-14, 211, 212
Horneck, 179, 180
Howley, Archbishop, 17
Hutchinson, 77
Hutton's 'Anglican Ministry,' 39, 51, 88

James I., King, 107, 108
James, Dr. T., 114
Jewell, Bishop, 80, 229
Johnson, John, 6, 37, 198, 199

Ken, Bishop, 13
Kennion, 3
Kettlewell, 177, 178
Kidder, Bishop, 186

Lake, Bishop, 117
Laney, Bishop, 169
Lathbury, 'History of Nonjurors,' 39, 72, 134
Lathbury, 'History of Convocation,' 134
Laud, Archbishop, 30, 31, 56, 128-131
Law, 220
Lawrence, 208
Lee, Dr. F. G., 56
Leighton, 170
Leriensis, 62
Leslie, 198
Lessius, 233
L'Estrange, 156, 157
Longley, Archbishop, 20

Mason, 104, 105
Mede, Joseph, 6, 121, 122
Mendham, 62

Index of Authorities

Meyer, 120, 241
Meyrick, Canon, 3
Montague, Bishop, 28, 30, 131
Morality of Tractarianism, 50
Morley, Bishop, 11, 172, 173
Morton, Bishop, 118, 119
Moule, 228

Neale's 'History of Puritans,' 30
Newman, Cardinal, 22, 23, 52, 58, 66-68
Nicholls, 213
Nicholson, Bishop, 161, 162
Nicole, 41
Nowell, Dean, 85
Nuncios, The Pope's, 28, 31

Overall, 3-6
Overall's Convocation Book, 4, 5

'Panzani Memoirs,' 28-30
'Papists not misrepresented,' 192
Parker, Archbishop, 5, 6, 84, 225, 228
Patrick, Bishop, 186, 187
Patrick, Dr. John, 189, 190
Payne, 179
Perkins, 230
Perry's 'History of Church of England,' 28, 134
Perry's 'Declaration on Kneeling,' 227
Phillpotts, Bishop, 50
Pilkington, 84, 85
Plumptre's 'Life of Ken,' 13
Pocklington, 140, 141
Potter, Archbishop, 219, 220
Prideaux, Bishop, 138
Prynn's 'Canterbury's Doom,' 28

Puller, 174
Pusey, Dr., 34, 35, 40, 41, 47

Reynolds, Bishop, 169
Ridley, 77, 228
Rogers, 98, 99
Routh, Dr., 23

Salmeron, 61, 236-240
Sancta Clara, 50, 55, 56
Sancroft, Archbishop, 10, 11
Sanderson, Bishop, 8, 144, 145
Sandys, Archbishop, 86, 87
Sarpi, 62
Scrivener, 170
Secker, Archbishop, 221
Sharp, Archbishop, 197
Sherlock, Dean, 190
Smith (Non-juror), 39
Soames, 227
Sparrow, Bishop, 171
Spinkes, 27, 201
Stillingfleet, 182-184, 190, 191
Strype, 81, 82, 225
Sutcliffe, 115

Taylor, Bishop Jeremy, 9, 10, 158, 159
'Testimony of Antiquity,' 84, 225
Theiner, 62
Thirlwall, Bishop, 57-59
Thorndike, H., 36, 167, 168
Tillotson, Archbishop, 176, 177
Tomline, Bishop, 223, 224
Towerson, 175
'Tracts for the Times,' No. 81, 3, 7, 33, 35-37
Tyndale, 73

Ussher, Archbishop, 7, 134, 135, 228

Vasquez, 233
Vencer, 219
'Vendiciæ Ecclesiæ Anglicanæ,' by W. T., 132
Viva, 234

Wake, 205-208, 229
Warburton, 222 [218
Waterland, 38, 39, 131, 215-
Welchman, 213, 214
Whateley, Archbishop, 50
Whitaker, 89
White, Bishop, 139, 140
Whitgift, 6, 90, 91

Willet, 99, 100
Williams, Archbishop John, 138, 139
Williams, Bishop Griffith, 127, 128
Williams, Bishop John, 193
Wood's 'Athenæ Oxonienses,' 57
Wordsworth, Bishop C., 16-19
Wren, Bishop, 157, 158
W. T., 132

Zurich Letters, 228

CORRIGENDA.

Page 27, line 10, *add* 'See also below, pp. 100, 105, 106, 117, 122, 129, 143, 144, 154, 155, 163-165, 187, 207.'
„ 30, „ 9, *for* 'Apello' *read* 'Appello.'
„ 49, „ 9 from bottom (note), *for* 'himself' *read* 'herself,' and *for* 'he' *read* 'she.'
„ 62, „ 2, *for* '1612' *read* '1602' and *add* 'See Appendix, Note C.'
„ 63, Note, line 6 from bottom, *for* 'propitiation' *read* 'propitiatory.'
„ 64, line 5, *for* 'Ante' *read* 'Anti.'
„ 93, „ 3 from bottom, *for* 'scholics' *read* 'scholies.'
„ 131, „ 4, *for* 'Trials' *read* 'Trial.'
„ 135, „ 7, *for* 'Ebrington' *read* 'Elrington.'
„ 163, „ 3 from bottom *add* 'See also pp. 282, 289, 290.'

THE END.

Price 3s. 6d. *net.*

'DANGEROUS DECEITS:'

AN EXAMINATION OF THE TEACHING OF OUR ARTICLE XXXI.

By Rev. N. DIMOCK, A.M.

' Mr. Dimock . . . has recently discussed the whole question with much ability and moderation.'—*Bishop of Worcester's Charge.*

'A very able vindication of the statement of our Thirty-first Article, that "the Sacrifices of Masses . . . were blasphemous fables and dangerous deceits." . . . We admire the wisdom and charity displayed in this treatise.'—*Record.*

'No one is better qualified than Mr. Dimock, by an exact and full knowledge of the Eucharistic controversy, to vindicate the meaning of "our Article." . . . The appearance of his vindication is most timely, and the task has been accomplished with marked ability. The book should henceforth form part of the library of every professional teacher who claims an acquaintance with the current errors of his own day. —*Church Intelligencer.*

' Mr. Elliot Stock publishes " Dangerous Deceits," an examination of the Thirty-first Church of England Article by Rev. N. Dimock, A.M., in which the author with unusual learning expounds the Protestant attitude towards the Mass.'—*Expositor.*

'Mr. Dimock goes thoroughly into the verbal and historical evidence, and has most industriously collected numerous quotations to illustrate his argument. Among the points on which the results of his labour can be examined with advantage are the precarious nature of the contention that " the doctrine of masses " and " the doctrine of the Mass " are widely different, the bearing of the dates of the Articles and the decrees of Trent, not only on the relation of the Articles to the Council of Trent in general, and the useful catena of the statements of English divines in the appendix.' *Guardian.*

ELLIOT STOCK, 62, PATERNOSTER ROW.

BY THE SAME AUTHOR.

CURIOSITIES OF PATRISTIC AND MEDIÆVAL LITERATURE. Nos. I. and II.
Price 3d. each.

THE DOCTRINE OF THE DEATH OF CHRIST.
Price 7s. 6d.

THE HOUR OF HOLY COMMUNION.
Price 6d.

THE EUCHARIST CONSIDERED IN ITS SACRIFICIAL ASPECT.
Price 3d.

SOME RECENT TEACHINGS CONCERNING THE EUCHARISTIC SACRIFICE.
A REVIEW.
Price 6d.

THE APOSTOLIC FATHERS AND THE CHRISTIAN MINISTRY.
A REVIEW.
Price 3d.

THE THEOLOGY OF BISHOP ANDREWES.
Price 3d.

ELLIOT STOCK, 62, PATERNOSTER ROW.

BY THE SAME AUTHOR.

THE DOCTRINE OF THE LORD'S SUPPER: TWO LECTURES WITH APPENDIX ON THE AUGMENTATION THEORY.

Price 2s. 6d.
ELLIOT STOCK.

THE 'EGO BERENGARIUS,' IN RELATION TO THE DEVELOPMENT OF THE DOCTRINE OF THE EUCHARIST.

Price 2s.
ELLIOT STOCK.

THE ROMISH MASS AND THE ENGLISH CHURCH.

Price 2s. 6d. In cloth, 3s. 6d.

ON EUCHARISTIC WORSHIP IN THE ENGLISH CHURCH.

Price 6s. 6d.

ON ARTICLE XXIX., DEALING WITH THE LETTERS OF GUESTE AND CECIL.

Price 1s.
[NOTE.—This is No. 8 of the following.]

PAPERS ON THE DOCTRINE OF THE ENGLISH CHURCH CONCERNING THE EUCHARISTIC PRESENCE.

Price 7s. 6d.

THE DOCTRINE OF THE SACRAMENTS IN RELATION TO THE DOCTRINES OF GRACE.

Price 5s. 6d.

MAIDSTONE: VIVISH.   EASTBOURNE: PULSFORD.
Post free on application.

www.ingramcontent.com/pod-product-compliance
Lightning Source LLC
Chambersburg PA
CBHW021410230426
43666CB00006B/697